THE MAGICIAN'S
WORKBOOK

THE MAGICIAN'S WORKBOOK

A MODERN GRIMOIRE

STEVE SAVEDOW

SAMUEL WEISER, INC.

York Beach, Maine

First published in 1995 by
Samuel Weiser, Inc.
P. O. Box 612
York Beach, ME 03910-0612

Library of Congress Cataloging-in-Publication Data
Savedow, Steve.
    Magician's workbook : a modern grimoire / Steve
    Savedow.
        p.   cm.
    Includes bibliographical references and index.
    1. Magic.   I. Title.
    BF1611.S28   1995
    133.4's—dc20   94–49077
                                              CIP

ISBN 0–87728–823–2
BJ

Typeset in 11 point Palatino

Printed in the United States of America

00 99 98
10 9 8 7 6 5 4 3 2

This book is dedicated to the memory of Samuel Ginsburg; with thanks to my lovely wife, Elaine, as well as Jacqueline, Barry, Belle, Sarah, and Melissa. Also, special thanks to Mary for posing in the yoga positions.

CONTENTS

Magic: pretended art of controlling events by charms, spells and rituals supposed to govern certain natural or supernatural forces.

Celestial Magic: a form of magic which attributes to spirits a kind of dominion over the planets and to the planets an influence over men.

Natural Magic: the art of employing the powers of nature to produce effects apparently supernatural.

—*Webster's New 20th Century Dictionary*, 1978

Magick is the Science and Art of causing Change to occur in conformity with Will.

—Aleister Crowley
Magick in Theory and Practice, 1929

INTRODUCTION

A *grimoire* is essentially a book of ritual magick. It may educate the reader as to how to perform ritual, or just outline a number of rituals written by the author. This book does both of those things.

It is my intention to provide the reader with an efficient, working manual to use in the practice of ritual magick. The earlier chapters in this text are directed toward the novice practitioner or beginner. Some chapters may appear too elementary for serious students who may have studied for a number of years, but the greater portion of this book should be very useful to even the long-time practitioner. Also, the elementary material could prove most useful to adepts, especially if they are teaching others.

Most of my viewpoints and methods are derived from a longtime study of the works of Aleister Crowley, S. L. MacGregor-Mathers, Eliphas Levi, Golden Dawn material, John Dee's Enochian material, *The Key of Solomon the King*, and other reputable grimoires.

The tasks set forth in these pages may well prove to be of great difficulty, and some readers will not possess the motivation or determination to accomplish them. But for those who are willing, worlds never before imagined, and secrets never before expressed are waiting. The mysteries of the universe lie at our feet. All that we must do is bend over backward—and reach for them.

Throughout this text I have used quotes from Aleister Crowley, who was probably the most influential, infamous, and noteworthy occult author of this century. I use his words simply because his eloquence on certain subjects is unmatched by any others in the field. Most of these quotes are from a book many consider to be Crowley's greatest work, *Magick in Theory and Practice*, first published in Paris in 1929. This work of Crowley's was originally meant as a textbook of ritual magick.[1] However, his brilliance was often masked by his subtlety, and much of his theory has been misinterpreted by the profane, or just plain confuses the uneducated. Also, the manner of speaking in England at the turn of the century was a bit more complex than today's modern American literature, and can be quite difficult for the young practitioner of the 1990's to assimilate. Crowley claimed that he had "published the most important practical magical secrets in the plainest language; no one, by virtue of being clever or learned, has understood one word; and those unworthy who have profaned the sacrament have but eaten and drunken damnation to themselves."[2]

The student will be in need of several notebooks,[3] and a great deal of paper and writing tools. These will be required to keep extensive records of all experiments, and results produced. One such notebook should consist of the records of the dates, times, and detailed descriptions of any interesting dreams, astral experiences, and all magickal rituals performed. This may include results, revelations, occurrences, experiences during meditation, poetry, and any magick-related experiences. No rituals should be left

---

[1] In fact, it was Crowley himself who added the "k" to the word "magic" so as to distinguish the word from that of "illusionary" magic, such as practiced by the entertaining stage performers who amuse the public with card tricks, and by pulling rabbits from hats.

[2] *Magick in Theory and Practice*, chapter 18.

[3] Three-ring binders are ideal.

out, if only to document the date, time, and type of operation. A separate notebook should be kept to record detailed outlines of all rituals that you perform. Still more notebooks will be required, as will be discussed in chapters 4, 11, and 18. The student of ritual magick is just that, a student, and will be expected to study the material provided as if preparing to be tested in the future, and believe me, you will be!

THE MAGICIAN'S
WORKBOOK

CHAPTER 1

INVOCATION AND EVOCATION

The two supreme acts of ritual magick are the invocation and the evocation. Webster defines "invocation" as "a formula for conjuring," and to "invoke" "to call forth by incantation." It defines "evocation" as "the summoning of a spirit," and "evoke" "to call forth or up" or to "conjure."[1] From these brief definitions, the two acts sound very similar, when in fact, they are extremely different. Indeed, both acts involve an interaction with nonhuman entities, however, the type of entity and the manner of interaction are vastly different during each of the separate acts. To really understand the difference between the two, it becomes necessary to grasp the concept of "hierarchy."

Hierarchy is essentially the "chain of command" for sentient beings. In the army, the chain of command is a system of titles or ranks designating executive positions, in order of authority.[2] In the "Magickal Universe," hierarchy involves the designation of "God" as the highest authority, and human beings being one of the lower. The full order of hierarchy is God, Demi-Gods, Archangels, angels, humans. Beneath human beings are the "spirits," or demons and archdemons. Beneath these demons are the most foul and loathsome creatures, and should not be of concern to the student, at this time.[3]

---

[1] *Webster's Ninth New Collegiate Dictionary* (Springfield, MA: Merriam-Webster, 1989).

[2] With a "general" being the highest authority, and a "private" being the lowest.

[3] Advanced students of the art will undoubtedly disagree immediately with this depiction of the universal hierarchy. I offer that this explanation is directed toward novices, and hopefully enables them to grasp what most would consider an extremely abstract concept. The "true" and complete hierarchy is much more of a vast, complex system than the simple "ladder" skeleton structure illustrated in figure 1 (page 2). It involves a myriad of individual beings, and its outline would be extremely difficult for the novice to interpret.

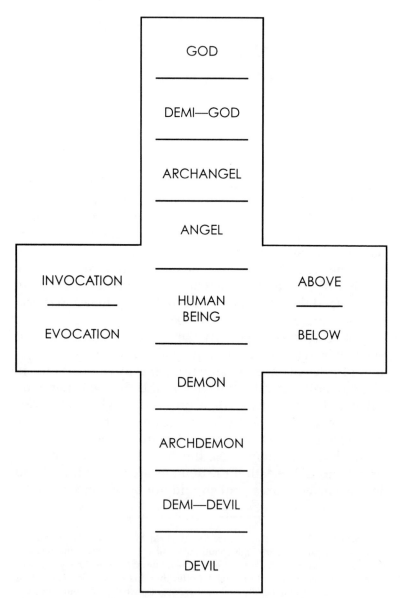

Figure 1. The Ladder of Hierarchy.

Knowing this system of hierarchy, it should be understood that invocation involves interaction with beings above us in the hierarchy, and evocation deals with the beings below.[4] The difference in the manner of interaction being that invocation is a request to the higher beings, and evocation is a demand to the lower beings. Invocations involve serenades, courtesy, love, and even sublimation. Evocations require curses and constraints, disdain, and occasionally, torture. Lastly, an invocation results in enticing a celestial influence into the circle, where an evocation forces the reluctant, repugnant demon out to the triangle. This should make it clear that these two acts are very different operations of what is known as "high" magick.

Allegorically speaking, the art of magick may be divided into two categories, that of high magick and that of low magick. There are instances where various writers hypothesize about the origins and meanings of the designations to some works as being "high" or "low." Some have said that it may have been due to the location of the practitioner, meaning that in the "highlands," the mighty court sorcerer would practice ritual magick, high up in the castles and courts of the royalty of the land, using weapons of steel and gold. While in the "lowlands," the impoverished witches practiced their craft in meager surroundings, utilizing wooden tools and roots and herbs that could be easily foraged for in the forests. Were this true, the classification of high and low magick would represent prejudice and injustice, suggesting that a "witch" would be incapable of practicing high magick. Fortunately, nothing could be further from the truth.

---

[4]Of course, there are those beings both above and below, who are beyond the means of a mere human being to either command or entice.

Witchcraft, or "wicca" as it is referred to today, may be described as a pagan religion of nature. Wicca is presently undergoing an upsurge of popularity, thanks to the relatively recent repeal of the infamous witchcraft laws,[5] that for centuries proclaimed the practice of paganism as "satanic."[6] Again, nothing could be further from the truth, which the groundbreaking writings of such wiccans as Gerald Gardner, Doreen Valiente and Sybil Leek, to mention just a few, have documented. Additionally, a background of wiccan beliefs is an excellent foundation to build a working knowledge and understanding of ritual magick upon.

The actual classification of distinguishing high magick from that of low magick should be based on the following criteria:

1) Low magick is performed in order to produce effects on the material plane, which is considered a "lower" plane. This includes such magick as love spells, money spells, good fortune spells, spells to improve crops, healings, curses, invisibility spells, and any operation that affects life on the physical or material plane.

2) High magick consists of essentially invocations and evocations. These operations have results that affect the higher or mental planes. They should compel the individual to progress emotionally, mentally, spiritually, and most importantly, magickally.[7]

As the results of high magick have a much greater potential for experience and meaning, so can they result in much

---

[5]In 1951.

[6]It should be noted that a satanist is essentially a Catholic/Christian person gone bad. These people believe firmly that God is the ultimate of supreme goodness, and that the "devil" is the supreme evil; and since they consider themselves "evil," their rightful allegiance belongs with the devil.

[7]It should be noted that a banishing ritual is technically considered a reverse invocation, and all rituals of high magick consist of first, a banishing, and second, an invocation, and if the operation calls for an evocation, it shall be third.

greater, and even disastrous, perils when improperly practiced. Failures in the works of low magick could conceivably cause unpleasant, and even painful repercussions on the material plane. But failures in the works of high magick can result in such forms as spiritual and emotional regression, mental deterioration, schizophrenia, psychosis, and insanity. For this reason, students of ritual magick should undertake a lengthy preparation period[8] which entails intensive study of certain texts that will be outlined in chapter 3. Additionally, extensive practices of certain exercises outlined in chapters 4–9 have been designed to prepare the uninitiated for future life as ritual magicians.

---

[8]Preferably, a period of one year.

Chapter 2

RITUAL CONSTRUCTION

Generally speaking, every ritual of high magick is composed of four periods of time. These are: creation, preparation, the performance and the results. The period of creation begins with either the "creation" of the ritual by the practitioner personally, or the discovery of a ritual, long lost or newly published. This is the point when the magician first realizes that the ritual must be performed. The "creation," or creative period, ends when the full ritual is laid out in detail on paper, in its entirety, to be studied and memorized during the next period.

The preparation period consists of finding a suitable location, gathering all necessary materials required for the ritual, and memorizing every detail of the ritual instructions. Additionally, a date and time must be selected when astrological influences would be favorable for this particular ritual. Many rituals require periods of fasting, sexual abstinence, long periods of meditation in solitude, devotions, daily banishings, etc.

The preparation period ends with the construction of the ritual area, which should be completed not more than twenty-four hours before the beginning of the "performance." The following are the lengthy rituals for the formation and construction of the circle, from *The Key of Solomon the King*[1]

---

[1]Translated by S. L. MacGregor-Mathers in 1888. This book is available today from Samuel Weiser, York Beach, ME.

Book II, chapter IX:

> Having chosen a place for preparing and constructing the Circle, and all things necessary being prepared for the perfection of the Operations, take thou the Sickle or Scimitar of Art and stick it into the centre of the place where the Circle is to be made; then take a cord of nine feet in length, fasten one end thereof unto the Sickle and with the other end trace out the circumference of the Circle, which may be marked either with the Sword or the Knife with the Black Hilt. Then

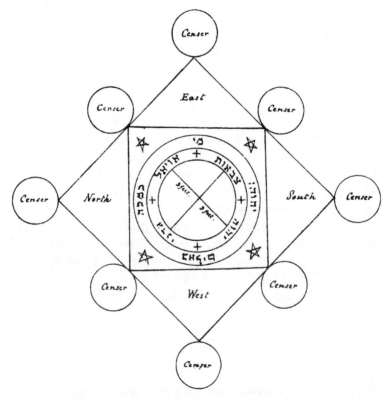

Figure 2. A Magic Circle, from *The Key of Solomon the King,* by S. L. MacGregor-Mathers.

within the Circle mark out four regions, namely, towards the East, West, South and North, wherein place symbols; and beyond the limits of this Circle describe with the Consecrated Knife or Sword another Circle, but leaving an open place therein towards the North whereby thou mayest enter and depart beyond the Circle of Art. Beyond this again thou shalt describe another Circle at a foot distance with the aforesaid Instrument, yet ever leaving therein an open space for entrance and egress corresponding to the open space already left in the other. Beyond this again make another

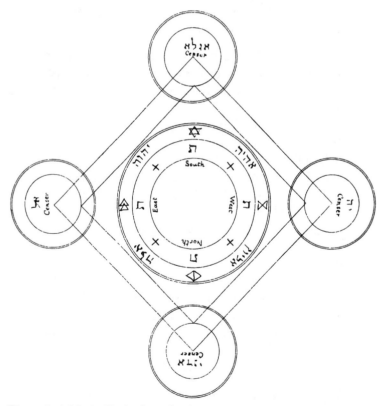

Figure 3. A Magic Circle, from the frontispiece of *The Key of Solomon the King*, by S. L. MacGregor-Mathers.

Circle at another foot distance, and beyond these two Circles, which are beyond the Circle of Art yet upon the same Centre, thou shalt describe Pentagrams with the Symbols and Names of the Creator therein so that they may surround the Circle already described. Without these Circles shalt thou circumscribe a Square, and beyond that another Square, so that the Angles of the former may touch the centres of the sides of the latter, and that the Angles may stretch towards the four quarters of the Universe, East, West, North and South; and at the four Angles of each square, and touching them , thou shalt describe lesser Circles wherein let there be placed standing censers with lighted charcoal and sweet odours.

These things being done, let the Magus of Art assemble his Disciples, exhort, confirm, and cheer them; lead them into the Circle of Art and station them therein towards the Four Quarters of the Universe, exhort them to fear nothing, and to abide in their assigned places. Furthermore, let each of the Companions have a Sword besides the Sword of the Art, which he must hold naked in his hand. Then let the Magus quit the Circle, and Kindle the Censers, and place thereon exorcised Incense, as is said in the Chapters of Fumigation; and let him have the Censer in his hand and kindle it, and then place it in the part prepared. Let him now enter within the Circle and carefully close the openings left in the same, and let him again warn his Disciples, and take the Trumpet of Art prepared as is said in the Chapter concerning the same, and let him incense the Circle towards the Four Quarters of the Universe.

After this let the Magus commence his Incantations, having placed the Sickle, Sword, or other

Implement of Art upright in the ground at his feet. Having sounded the trumpet as before taught let him invoke the Spirits, and if need be conjure them, as is said in the First Book, and having attained his desired effect, let him license them to depart.

Here followeth the Form of the Circle (see figure 2) wherein whosoever entereth he shall be at safety as within a fortified Castle, and nothing shall be able to harm him.

Book I, chapter III:

Take thou the Knife, the Sickle, or the Sword of Magical Art consecrated after the manner and order which we shall deliver unto thee in the Second Book. With this Knife or with the Sickle of Art thou shalt describe, beyond the inner Circle which thou shalt have already formed, a Second Circle, encompassing the other at the distance of one foot therefrom and having the same centre.[2] Within this space of a foot in breadth between the first and second circumferential line[3] thou shalt trace towards the Four Quarters of the Earth[4] the Sacred and Venerable Symbols of the holy Letter Tau[5] and between the first and second Circle,[6] which thou shalt thyself have drawn with the Instrument of Magickal Art, thou shalt make four

---

[2]From *The Key of Solomon*: two Circles enclosed between three circumferential lines.
[3]From *The Key of Solomon*: within the first Circle.
[4]From *The Key of Solomon*: The four Cardinal points of the compass.
[5]From *The Key of Solomon*: The letter Tau represents the Cross, and in I0862 Add. MSS. in the drawing of the Circle, the Hebrew letter is replaced by the Cross; in I307 Sloane MSS. by the T or Tau-Cross.
[6]From *The Key of Solomon*: In the outer Circle, bounded by the second and third circumferential lines.

hexagonal pentacles,[7] and between them thou shalt write four terrible and tremendous Names of God, viz.:

> Between the East and the South the Supreme Name IHVH, Tetragrammaton;
> Between the South and the West the Essential Tetragrammatic Name AHIH, Eheih;
> Between the West and the North the Name of Power ALIVN, Elion;
> And between the North and the East the Great Name ALH, Eloah;
> Which Names are of supreme importance in the list of the Sephiroth,[8] and their Sovereign Equivalents.

Furthermore, thou shalt circumscribe about these Circles two Squares, the Angles of which shall be turned towards the Four Quarters of the Earth; and the space between the Lines of the Outer and Inner Square shall be half-a-foot. The extreme Angles of the Outer Square shall be made the Centres of four Circles, the measure or diameter of which shall be one foot. All of these are to be drawn with the Knife or consecrated Instrument of Art. And within these Four Circles thou must write these four Names of God the Most Holy One, in this order:

> At the East, AL, El:
>
> At the West, IH, Yah;

---

[7]From *The Key of Solomon*: I0862 Add. MSS. is the only copy which uses the word *hexagonal*, but the others show four hexagrams in the drawing; in the drawing, however, I0862 gives the hexagrams formed by various differing interlacements of two triangles.

[8]From *The Key of Solomon*: The Sephiroth are the ten Qabalistic Emanations of the Deity. The Sovereign Equivalents are the Divine Names referred thereto.

At the South, AGLA, Agla;

And at the North ADNI, Adonai.[9]

Between the two Squares the Name Tetragrammaton is to be written in the same way as is shown in the plate [see figure 3 on page 9.]

While constructing the Circle, the Master should recite the following Psalms: Psalm II; Psalm LIV; Psalm CXII; Psalm LXVII; Psalm XLVII; Psalm LXVIII.

Or he may as well recite them before tracing the Circle.

The which being finished, and the fumigations being performed, as is described in the chapter on Fumigations in the Second Book, the Master should assemble his Disciples, encourage them, reassure them, fortify them, and conduct them into the parts of the Circle of Art, where he must place them at the Four Quarters of the Earth, encourage them, and exhort them to fear nothing, and to keep in the places assigned to them. Also, the Disciple who is placed toward the East should have a pen, ink, paper, silk and white cotton, all clean and suitable for the work. Furthermore, each of the Companions should have a new Sword drawn in his hand (in addition to consecrated Magical Sword of Art), and he should keep his hand resting upon the hilt thereof, and he should on no pretext quit the place assigned to him, nor move therefrom.

After this the Master should quit the Circle, light the fuel in the earthen pots, and place

---

[9]From *The Key of Solomon*: The MSS. vary as to the point whereat each Name is to be placed, but I think the above will be found to answer.

upon them the Censers, in the Four Quarters of the Earth; and he should have in his hand the consecrated taper of wax, and he should light it and place it in a hidden and secret place prepared for it. Let him after this re-enter and close the Circle.

The Master should afresh exhort his Disciples, and explain to them all they have to do and to observe; the which commands they should promise and vow to execute. Let the Master then repeat this Prayer:[10]

What follows this is two prayers and one conjuration before the completion of the ritual. This is only one of many difficult tasks one needs to fulfill, before practicing ritual detailed in *The Key of Solomon*. All prerequisites outlined in this ancient grimoire should be completed before attempting any operation of Solomon's Art; otherwise the results will reflect the inadequacies, and may well end in disaster. For this reason, it would probably be impractical for most people to practice from this grimoire. In general, however, one should not be deterred from performing a ritual because of the difficulty of the preparation period. Objects needed may be difficult to locate or construct, and memorizing an in-depth ritual may take weeks or even months; but the effort exerted during this preparation only adds to the energy of the ritual. The energy generated begins with the initial creation, and continues building even after the performance is completed. One's sheer determination is an intricate key to the success of a ritual. The next chapter of this book deals extensively with preparation, as this is actually the most important part of ritual construction.

The performance of the ritual begins at the specific date and time determined well in advance according to

---

[10]*The Key of Solomon the King*, pp. 17–18.

favorable astrological influences. The first act should begin with a ritual bathing or cleansing, outside of the designated ritual area. Traditionally, using natural water (ocean or spring water, preferably) treated with a small amount of hyssop, and the particular herbal oil suitable to the nature of the ritual.[11] This act of bathing represents the purification of the magician, and at some point while bathing, these words should be spoken:

> Asperges me, EHIEH, hyssopo, et mundabor; lavabis me, et super nivem dealbabor.

After the ritual bathing and before donning the robe, the magician should use the right forefinger to make the mark of the "Rose Cross"[12] over the heart with Abramelin oil[13] while speaking these words of consecration:

> Accendat in nobis ADONAI ignem sui amoris et flammam aeternae caritatis.

This represents the second act of the ritual.[14]

The robe should be donned before entering the ritual area, and all magical weapons/tools should have been prepared well in advance, and left waiting on the altar within the circle area.[15] Every magickal tool or weapon, including the altar and the robe, must be first purified by sprinkling

---

[11]For example, a solar working would suggest the use of frankincense, and jasmine would be recommended for a lunar working.

[12]See figure 9 in chapter 4.

[13]A mixture of cinnamon, myrrh and galangal oil.

[14]Both the words of purification and consecration are from chapter 14 of *Magick in Theory & Practice* by Aleister Crowley, and were deriveed from *The Key of Solomon*. Additionally, the capitalized words EHIEH and ADONAI are meant to be "vibrated," which will be described in chapter 4.)

[15]A black robe, of either cotton or silk, is always suitable for the uninitiated, although it may also be of benefit to use a colored robe, one which would reflect the nature of the ritual, preferably in the King and Queen colors qabalistically.

each with hyssop-treated natural water while speaking the words of purification, and then consecrated by rubbing it with Abramelin oil, while speaking the words of consecration.[16] This procedure should be completed no more than twelve hours prior to any magickal operation.

The third act of the performance should be to perform the banishing ritual, several of which are outlined in chapter 4. These three acts should be performed before the "main" performance, that of the specific ritual itself.

The main ritual and all preliminaries and closings are performances, and should be theatrical and powerfully performed. Be sure your location allows this necessity. It would not do at all to whisper your incantations, so as not to disturb the neighbors.

The final acts of the performance are the closing "banishing ritual," the "release of the spirits," and the "closing of the temple." This signifies the completion of the ritual, and traditionally ends with a single rap on the top of the altar with the butt of the ritual dagger. Thereafter, the magician should leave the circle area, not to return for at least one hour. The magician should then return, remove all evidence of the ritual, and banish the area once again.

The fourth period of time begins at the moment of the final release of the performance, as the circle is closed. It is of utmost importance that your expected results are not considered, or even thought of during the preparation and performance of the ritual. The desired results should be recorded during the creation of the ritual on a separate page, and then hidden away to be forgotten. At some point after the results of your ritual are experienced, the page may be retrieved and compared with the actual results. The actual results should be recorded, and the two pages may then be placed in your magical records.

It is vital to realize that your own expectation of results during the preparation period or performance will either

---

[16]Chapter 11 deals with the magickal weapons in detail.

completely hinder or even alter the actual results of the act—virtually ruining the experiment—for the results should be what was originally desired at the first moment of creation. Any deviation of the original expected results would render the operation unsuccessful. For this reason, it is advisable to concentrate all energies on the performance of the ritual itself, while completely blocking out the original intention of the ritual.

Chapter 3

PREPARATION FOR THE RITUAL MAGICIAN

The success of any magical ritual is dependent on the preparation of the magician performing. One who is not completely and undeniably fit to perform will fail. If only one small detail is left unfinished, the operation will fail. There can be no doubt about the fact that everything must be perfect when performing magical ritual. No substitutions are allowed, and no questions go unanswered. Any imperfection will magnify under the stress of ritual; so before proceeding with the performance, be absolutely positive that all is as it should be.

Stamina is important to ritual, especially in evocationary work. One must prepare the body physically before even considering performing ritual. Being either underweight or overweight is detrimental physically, as well as dangerous magically. The magician should take (at least) a good multiple vitamin daily, exercise regularly, and should ideally fit into the following weight categories listed in Table 1 on page 20.[1]

The aspiring magician should have the ability to run a mile briskly without keeling over, and be able to lift his or her body weight up to chest level without injury. Again, these are not requirements, but to surpass these informal suggestions is unquestionably desirable.

It may well take a good amount of time to prepare yourself to begin to practice ritual magick, but to undergo ritual unprepared is dangerous and foolhardy, and will

---

[1]These are not requirements. However, if you do not fall into these categories, it is recommended that you strive to.

Table 1. Ideal Weights.

MALES		FEMALES	
Height	Weight	Height	Weight
5′–5′3″	110lb–140lb	5′–5′3″	90lb–120lb
5′4″–5′6″	120lb–150lb	5′4″–5′6″	100lb–135lb
5′6″–5′9″	130lb–170lb	5′6″–5′9″	110lb–150lb
5′10″–6′	140lb–185lb	5′10″–6′	125lb–165lb

likely be regrettable. This is not an activity one should enter into lightly. It basically requires devotion to a lifelong study. It is no coincidence that all of the great "mythological" magicians are depicted as being very old, even ancient figures. The student will endure countless failures to catch a glimmer of success; but determination should be your driving force. Aleister Crowley chose "Perdurabo" as his motto for a time,[2] which translates, "I will endure to the end." It takes years of study and practice before you might record the smallest of encouraging results, but they can and will come in time. The first step you must take on this path may well be the most difficult, physically. This is the "preparation."

By following the instructions in the upcoming chapters, you will have placed your feet firmly on the Path of the Serpent. By practicing the appropriate exercises, and reading the proper texts, you will be preparing both body and mind to indulge in the art and science of magick. In a

---

[2]Every ritual magician should choose a "magickal motto." This should be a short statement, or even one word, which best expresses your intention or purpose for practicing magick. This may also be a statement of great significance, to you personally and/or magickally. The word or statement might sound impressive translated into a language which has a strong magickal heritage, such as Hebrew, Latin, or Greek. Many years ago, I chose: "In persequi semita de anquis," or "I.P.S.D.A." This translates, "To follow the path of the serpent." Other notable mottos include "Iehi Aour" (belonging to Allen Bennett, a colleague of Aleister Crowley, and translated from the Hebrew as "Let there be light"), "Sacramentum Regis" (belonging to Arthur E. Waite, and translated as "The sacrament of the King"), and "Deo Duce Comite Ferro" (belonging to S. L. MacGregor-Mathers, which translates as, "With God as my leader and the sword as my companion").

sense, ritual magick combines the documented facts of science with artistic qualities, which are outlined here:

ARTISTIC FACTORS

1) Writing of ritual, spells, incantations, etc.;

2) Performance of ritual;

3) Creation of magickal weapons;

4) Making of talismans, charms, etc.;

5) Creative visualizations;

6) Vibration of words;

7) Usage of colors, smells, sounds, etc.

SCIENTIFIC FACTORS

1) Study of various correspondences (Qabalistic, etc.);

2) Breakdown of Magickal formula;

3) Mathematics of Qabalah, Gematria, etc.;

4) Astrological surveys;

5) Study of ancient and foreign philosophy;

6) Knowledge of "alchemical" effects;

7) Use of various elements (chemistry) and their forces.

Very few fields may be classified as both an art and a science. The two usually oppose each other, but by bringing them together, a force greater than either individually is created. It is through the combination of many seemingly unrelated factors that magickal results are produced. These results will seem miraculous to the mundane, but the magician knows that they are simply acts of nature, based on the laws of cause and effect. Human beings are not aware of these laws instinctively; the laws must be learned, and if you continue to read these pages, learn you will!

Recommended Reading

It is taken for granted that you have already read books on this subject, but if you have not read *Book 4* and *Magick in Theory and Practice* by Aleister Crowley, then do so. Also recommended are *The Book of Ceremonial Magic*, or *The Book of Black Magic and Pacts*[3] by Arthur E. Waite, *Transcendental Magic: Its Doctrine and Ritual* by Eliphas Levi, and *The Magus or Celestial Intelligencer* by Francis Barrett. One could literally spend years studying these few books. Buy inexpensive copies suitable to make notes in, and underline passages. These are the textbooks for ritual magicians of our century.[4]

It is also recommended that you keep a notebook while studying these books, so you can record any pertinent revelations, impressions, interpretations, or enlightening thoughts you may experience while absorbing these texts.

You should continue reading this book through, and begin the practices and exercises which follow. Start locating the first titles listed here, and begin studying them, taking appropriate notes in the notebook dedicated to

---

[3]The two are the same book.

[4]Aleister Crowley, *Book Four*, (London: Wieland & Co., 1912; York Beach, ME: Samuel Weiser, 1980); Aleister Crowley, *Magic in Theory and Practice by the Master Therion* (Paris: LeCram Press, 1929; New York: Castle Books, n.d.; New York: Krishna Press, 1973; New York: Magickal Childe, 1991); Arthur E. Waite, *The Book of Black Magic and Pacts* (London, 1898; York Beach, ME: Samuel Weiser, 1972.) This book has also been published as *Book of Ceremonial Magic* (London: 1911; New York: Carol Publishing Group, 1970); Eliphas Levi, *Trancendental Magic: Its Doctrine and Ritual,* trans. by Arthur E. Waite (London: Rider, 1896; York Beach, ME: Samuel Weiser, 1968); Francis Barrett, *The Magus or Celestial Intelligencer: Being a Complete System of Occult Philosophy* (London: Lackington Allen Co., 1801; New York: University Book, 1967; New York: Citadel, 1975).

that purpose. Find copies of *Book 4* and *Magick in Theory and Practice*,[5] then take an hour or two daily to study them. Do not dwell too long in any one section, as you will be rereading these books many times in future years, before Crowley's words can be interpreted properly. Afterward, begin the same process with Waite's *Book of Ceremonial Magic*.[6] Continue in this manner through the other titles mentioned in the first paragraph of this chapter, and then keep repeating the process until you have a grasp of the theory discussed, all the while making appropriate notes, as if studying to be sternly tested on the material. Obviously, I will not be testing you, but this book should be considered a course on the subject, and if you take this subject seriously, study as if your future depended on it. If you plan on practicing this art, you may regret doing so without being fully educated in the field.

You will quickly realize that these books are not light reading. Read not more than ten pages at a time, and take a reflective break between sittings, to record thoughts, ideas, etc. If necessary, read the section twice, or even three times, before moving on to the next section. Underline or mark passages that have deep significance for you, or mark the passages you don't understand, so you may return to the section later.[7] The recommended reading list to follow could be an endless one, but it has been trimmed down to include just the essential works. Also, try to locate the titles mentioned by the authors of these recommended books.

---

[5] *Book 4* is actually parts 1 and 2 of a trilogy, in which *Magick in Theory and Practice* is part 3.

[6] There is no need to make a study of the lengthy quotes from the various grimoires in this book, although they are fascinating. For now, just read them through once, and concern yourself mainly with Waite's commentaries.

[7] Do not use early or antiquarian editions! Buy cheap reprints to make marks in.

Other Recommended Reading

Astral Projection, Ritual Magic & Alchemy (S. L. MacGregor-
Mathers)
The Black Arts (Richard Cavendish)
The Book of Splendours (Eliphas Levi)
Ceremonial Magic (Israel Regardie)
The Complete Golden Dawn System of Magic (Israel Regardie)
The Fourth Book of Occult Philosophy (Cornelius Agrippa)
The Golden Bough (James Frazer)
The Golden Dawn (Israel Regardie)
*The Great Book of Magical Art, Hindu Magic & Indian
Occultism* (L. W. DeLaurence)
The History of Magic (Eliphas Levi)
The Magical Revival (Kenneth Grant)
Magick Without Tears (Aleister Crowley)
Modern Ritual Magic (Francis King)
Natural Magic (John B. Porta)
The Secret Lore of Magic (Idries Shah)
Techniques of High Magic (Francis King)
Three Books of Occult Philosophy (Cornelius Agrippa)
True and Faithful Relation of Dr. John Dee (John Dee)
777 & Other Qabalistic Writings of Aleister Crowley (Aleister
Crowley)[8]

Reprint Editions of Reputable Grimoires

The Arbatel of Magic (trans. by Robert Turner)
The Book of the Sacred Magic of Abra-Melin the Mage (trans. by
S. L. MacGregor-Mathers)

---

[8]All titles by Aleister Crowley, including his fictional works, are highly recommended. Due to a certain lifelong influence, his writings are rich with magickal
symbolism.

The Key of Solomon the King (trans. by S. L. MacGregor-Mathers)

The Grimoire of Armadel (trans. by S. L. MacGregor-Mathers)

Lemegeton (trans. by Nelson White and Anne White)

The Goetia or Lesser Key of Solomon the King (trans. by Aleister Crowley)

The Secret Grimoire of Turiel (trans. by Marius Malchus)

The Sixth & Seventh Books of Moses (trans. by L. W. DeLaurence)

The Sworn Book of Honourius (trans. by Daniel J. Driscoll)

Although they make fascinating reading, it is not recommended to practice the rituals outlined in these grimoires, unless you can obtain all necessary accoutrements listed in the ritual, and every detail listed is exactly as described. This may prove nearly impossible for most, as most of these grimoires were written many hundreds of years ago, when certain materials were available that are virtually non-existent today.

CHAPTER 4

THE MIDDLE PILLAR
AND BANISHING RITUALS

It will likely take quite a while to study the books recommended in the previous chapter. Additionally, the aspiring magician should practice certain rituals at regular intervals of the day. In this chapter, there are outlines for five rituals. These are "The Middle Pillar Ritual," "The Lesser Banishing Ritual of the Pentagram," "The Lesser Banishing Ritual of the Hexagram," "The Banishing Ritual of the Serpent," and "The Star Ruby." Figures 4-11 on pages 30-37 illustrate aspects of these rituals.

Begin studying "The Middle Pillar Ritual," and memorize it. After you have this ritual memorized, copy it down in the front of what will become your personal "Book of Shadows," or magickal record. Perform this ritual in the morning and evening every day for a month. During the month, study and memorize "The Lesser Banishing Ritual of the Pentagram," and copy it into your records. After the first month, perform this ritual twice a day, just before "The Middle Pillar," for a month. Memorize and record the "Lesser Banishing Ritual of the Hexagram" during the second month, and perform it during the afternoon every day of the third month, still performing the first two twice daily. Repeat the process with "The Banishing Ritual of the Serpent" and "The Star Ruby," until you perform all five rituals at least once daily for a month. Try to maintain a steady schedule, performing each at around the same time every day. Since these are all relatively short rituals, the total time of practice should be only about an hour daily.

Certain words used in these rituals are to be "vibrated" by the performing magician. Musicians, people involved in the music business, and even music fans, are aware of physical reactions to sound. Besides the obvious pleasure many receive from listening to good music,[1] and age old sayings such as "Music hath charms to soothe the savage beast."[2] The ability of a singer to break a glass with a high note has been publically recorded on a number of occasions.[3]

The ability to vibrate your voice depends on a tonal quality known as "resonance." It is not loudness, or even authority which provides the vibration, as many may think. The vibration requires a changing of sound and pitch, caused by the erratic vibration of the larynx or voicebox, while speaking. In many cases, this may be accomplished by taking a very deep breath and slowly letting it out while singing the word in your highest voice, even encouraging the "cracking" of your voice. This may sound ridiculous at first, but results are what counts. The vibration should be felt in the throat while speaking or singing.

The words to be vibrated in the following rituals are in capitalized letters. They are of ancient Hebrew descent, except for those in "The Star Ruby," which are Greek; and most of them are termed "God-names" or "words of power."[4] These words are spelled for proper English pronunciation in the following outlines. Every sound of every letter should be vibrated individually, yet flowing into each other as one word.

It is believed that by vibrating the names described in the last paragraph in combination with the drawing of its corresponding symbol with your personal energy,[5] that you may cause certain effects to occur. In the case of banishing

---

[1] Or being saddened and depressed by the "blues".

[2] James Bramston.

[3] For example, Ella Fitzgerald.

[4] See Appendix A.

[5] Personal energy will be discussed extensively in chapter 6. For now, suffice it to say that personal energy is what makes up your aura, and when drawing symbols in ritual, you should see it as lines in the air appearing from your fingertips, or from the blade.

rituals, you are seeking to banish or remove unwanted influences from yourself or from your area of working. Specifically, elemental forces[6] in the case of the following rituals. Some elemental forces can influence you in undesirable ways, such as actually weakening or diluting your personal energy, due to their natural impurities. You are trying to cleanse your personal energy during these rituals.

The pentagram[7] and hexagram[8] are the symbols utilized in the following rituals. It is difficult to simply explain the technical symbolisms of these ancient symbols; however they may be studied in Regardie's *The Golden Dawn* in great detail. Suffice it to say that these rituals are ancient in their lineage, and have always managed to produce their desired effects, when properly performed.

Needless to say, drawing the symbols with your personal energy will involve seeing lines of energy that you create. To quote Aleister Crowley: "These rituals should be practiced until the figures drawn appear in flame, in flame so near to physical flame that it would perhaps be visible to the eyes of a bystander, were one present. It is alleged that some persons have attained the power of actually kindling fire by these means. Whether this be so or not, the power is not to be aimed at."[9]

When using a dagger for banishing, a double edged blade with a black handle is traditional.

"The Middle Pillar Ritual," "The Lesser Banishing Ritual of the Pentagram," and "The Lesser Banishing Ritual of the Hexagram" are of Golden Dawn descent. "The Banishing Ritual of the Serpent" was composed by the author, and "The Star Ruby" was composed by Aleister Crowley.[10]

---

[6]Which are considered impure in their natural states.

[7]The five-pointed star.

[8]The six-pointed star.

[9]"Liber O vel Manus et Sagittae" in *Magic in Theory and Practice*, p. 375. Crowley originally published this material in *The Equinox*, Vol. I, p. 11. A 1992 reprint of *The Equinox* is available from Samuel Weiser, York Beach, ME.

[10]"Liber XXV" in *Magick in Theory and Practice* (New York: Castle Books, n.d.) p. 327.

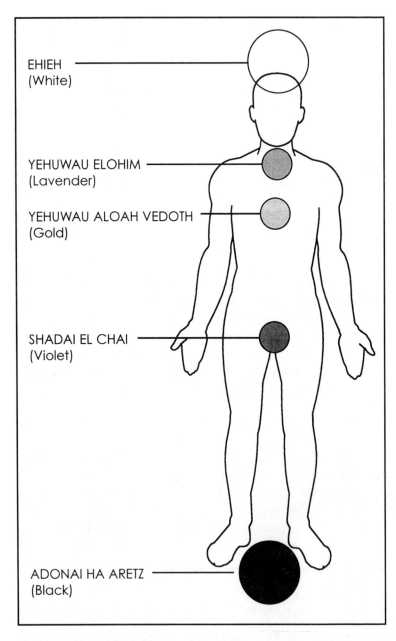

EHIEH
(White)

YEHUWAU ELOHIM
(Lavender)

YEHUWAU ALOAH VEDOTH
(Gold)

SHADAI EL CHAI
(Violet)

ADONAI HA ARETZ
(Black)

Figure 4. The Middle Pillar Ritual.

THE RENDING OF THE VEIL

THE CLOSING OF THE VEIL

THE GOD SHU
SUPPORTING THE SKY

THE GODDESS
THOUM-AESH-NEITH

THE GODDESS AURAMOTH

THE GOD SET FIGHTING

Figure 5. The Signs of the Portal and the Elemental Gods.

OSIRIS SLAIN

MOURNING OF ISIS

APOPHIS AND TYPHON

OSIRIS RISEN

Figure 6. The Signs of L. V. X.

PUER

VIR

PUELLA

MULIER

Figure 7. The Signs of N. O. X.

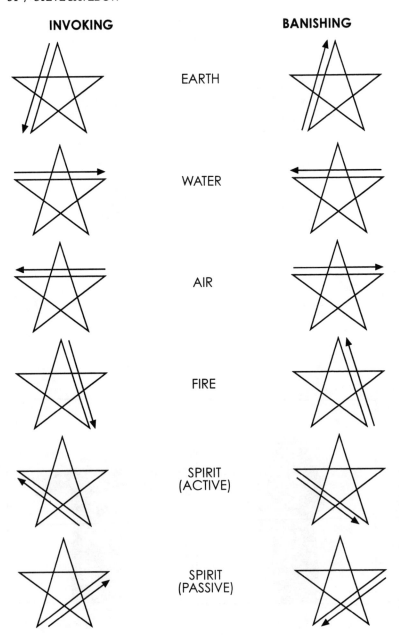

Figure 8. The Invoking and Banishing Pentagrams.

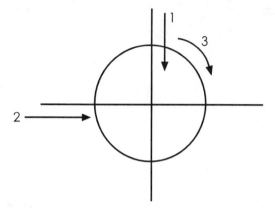

Figure 9. The Rose Cross.

THE SIGN OF
HARPOCRATES OR SILENCE

THE SIGN OF
HORUS OR THE ENTERER

Figure 10. Signs of Harpocrates and Horus.

INVOKING

BANISHING

FIRE

EARTH

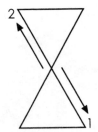
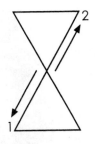

WATER

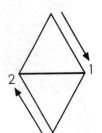
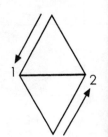

AIR

INVOKING   **BANISHING**

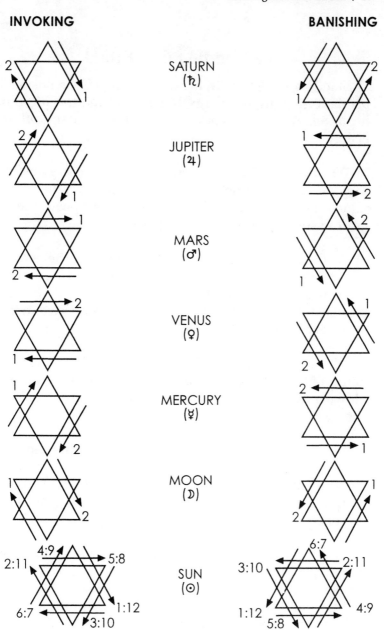

Figure 11. The Invoking and Banishing Hexagrams.

The Middle Pillar Ritual

1) Standing upright with hands by your sides, envision a brilliant glowing of energy building at the top of your head. See it as a glowing orb or ball of brilliant white energy.

2) When you can feel and see the glow of this energy building, vibrate the name EHIEH while concentrating your mind on that glowing ball at the top of your head. Feel it grow in strength as you vibrate the God name.

3) As the crown chakra glows overhead, feel the energy descend downwards as you begin to see and feel a lavender glowing at your throat level. Envision an orb or ball of lavender-colored energy, which should be connected to the orb above your head by a line of energy.

4) When you can see and feel this energy, vibrate the God name YEHUWAU ELOHIM, while concentrating on the glowing at your throat. Also take notice that the ball of energy is still building in energy.

5) As the two orbs continue to build in intensity, feel the energy descend once again while you envision a golden glow emanating from your heart area in the form of an orb of glowing energy. All should be connected by that same line of energy.

6) When you can see and feel this energy, vibrate the God name YEHUWAU ALOAH VEDOTH while concentrating on the glowing at your heart level. Feel it as it builds in intensity and strength. Notice that the other orbs are still building in intensity, and are all interconnected.

7) Next follow the same procedure at your genital level, except that you should envision the color of that energy as violet and vibrate the God name SHADAI EL CHAI.

8) Follow the same procedure at your feet, envisioning a deep black energy emanating from the ground around your feet, and vibrate the God name ADONAI HA ARETZ.

9) All of these orbs should remain interconnected by the line of energy, and "burning" with intensity and strength. Feel the energy flowing between them, permeating your body, and wrapping around you like a breeze or breath of air blowing over your skin. This should be quite an enjoyable feeling. Maintain it as long as you so desire.

See figure 4 on page 30 for an illustration of the Middle Pillar Ritual.

The Lesser Banishing
Ritual of the Pentagram

1) Stand in the center of the circle area and face the east.

2) Perform the Qabalistic Cross:

A. Hold dagger in both hands [if not using a dagger, place your thumb between the index and middle finger, and use just your right hand] and touch [or just come close] the forehead, while vibrating ATOH. Visualize a crystal blue glowing above and around your head.

B. Move the dagger downward to the breast area, defining a line of energy, and then vibrate MALKUTH.

C. Move dagger upward to the throat level, and then move horizontally to the right shoulder defining a line of energy, and vibrate VE GEBURAH.

D. Move the dagger horizontally across to the left shoulder, and vibrate VE GEDULAH.

E. Move the dagger horizontally to the throat, and then vertically downward to the breast level. Then hold the dagger pointing upward, and vibrate LE OLAHM, AUM. You should now be visualizing a cross upon your body. As you vibrate LE OLAHM, AUM, you should visualize yourself being enveloped by a sphere of crystal blue, almost clear energy. It begins enveloping you from where the dagger rests upon your breast, above your head and below your feet simultaneously, then joining behind you to form the sphere. This concludes the Qabalistic Cross.

3) Move forward [or to the left around the altar] to stand in the easternmost point of the circle, facing the east. With the

dagger in your right hand, draw the Banishing Pentagram of Earth while vibrating YEHUWAU. This pentagram should be approximately three feet in size, directly in front of you. After drawing the pentagram, thrust the dagger into its center with both hands.

4) After thrusting the dagger into the center of the pentagram, move deosil [clockwise], visually tracing a line with the dagger, to the southernmost point of the circle. Face the south and, with the dagger in your right hand, draw the Banishing Pentagram of Earth again, while vibrating ADONAI. Then thrust the dagger into the center with both hands.

5) Move as before, tracing a line to the westernmost point of the circle, and face the west. Then draw the Banishing Pentagram of Earth again while vibrating EHIEH. Then thrust the dagger into the center.

6) Move as before, tracing a line to the northernmost point of the circle, and face the north. Draw the Banishing Pentagram of Earth once more while vibrating AGLA. Thrust the dagger into its center, and then trace the line back to the eastern pentagram. Touch the dagger to its center, and then return to the center of the circle, facing the east. This completes the casting of the circle.

7) Then say "Before me stands [vibrates] RAFAEL, behind me stands GABRIEL, on my right side stands MICHAEL, and on my left stands AURIEL. For about me flames the pentagram, and within me burns the six-rayed star."

8) Still standing in the center and facing east, repeat the Qabalistic Cross.

See figure 8 on page 34 for the Invoking and Banishing Pentagrams.

The Lesser Banishing Ritual
of the Hexagram

1) Stand in the center of the circle area, and face the east.

2) Hold the dagger in your right hand at breast level, pointing upward. The left hand should be at your side. Then perform the analysis of I.A.O., saying:

> I.N.R.I.
>
> Yod Nun Resh Yod
>
> Virgo, Isis, Mighty Mother
>
> Scorpio, Apophis, Destroyer
>
> Sol, Osiris, Slain and Risen
>
> Isis, Apophis, Osiris
>
> [vibrate] IAO

3) Perform "The signs of L.V.X.":

[It would also be helpful to assume the God-forms corresponding to these deities, as described in Appendix B. The assumption of God-forms will be described in greater detail in chapter 8.]

> A. Extend your arms horizontally to form a cross, and say, "The sign of Osiris Slain" [See figure 6, p. 32].

> B. Form the letter "L" by extending your right arm horizontally, with the elbow bent at a ninety-degree angle, and forearm pointing upward. The left arm should be at your side. Turn your head to look down your left arm, and turn your right foot to point slightly inward, toe

touching ground and heel slightly raised. Then say "The sign of the mourning of Isis."

C. Raise both arms upward to form the letter "V," with feet together, standing up on toes, and head thrown back. Then say "The sign of Apophis and Typhon."

D. Cross your arms over your breast, right arm over left, and bow your head. Then say "The sign of Osiris Risen."

E. Extend arms as in Step 3-A, and say "L.V.X. Lux, the Light of the Cross."

4) Move forward to the easternmost point of the circle, and face the east. With the dagger in your right hand, draw the Banishing Hexagram of Fire, while vibrating ARARITA. This hexagram should be approximately three feet in size, directly in front of you. After drawing the hexagram, thrust the dagger into its center with both hands.

5) After thrusting the dagger into the center of the hexagram, move deosil, visually tracing a line to the southernmost point of the circle. Face the south and, with the dagger in your right hand, draw the Banishing Hexagram of Earth while vibrating ARARITA. Then thrust the dagger into its center with both hands.

6) Move as before, tracing a line to the westernmost point of the circle, and face the west. There draw the Banishing Hexagram of Air while vibrating ARARITA. Then thrust the dagger into the center as before.

7) Move as before, tracing a line to the northernmost point of the circle, and face the north. Then draw the Banishing Hexagram of Water while vibrating ARARITA. Thrust the dagger into its center, and then trace the line back to the

eastern hexagram, moving deosil. Touch the dagger to its center, and then return to the center of the circle, facing east.

8) Repeat steps 1 through 3.

See figure 11 on page 37 for the Invoking and Banishing Hexagrams.

The Banishing Ritual of the Serpent

1) While standing in the center of the circle area, face the east and say with force: "Attention all creatures within the range of this voice. BE AWARE that an act of Magick is about to be performed on this spot. ALL uninvited guests are advised to depart Now!"

2) Still standing in the center of the circle, facing east, lift your hands above your head, and say, "Fire falls down from out of the sky," while lowering your hands below your waist level. Then lift your hands upward toward your face level, and say, "And the Earth rises up." Then allow your hands to flow outward from your body, defining a circle, and they should meet again at your waist level. While making this gesture say, "But amidst all of the confusion, Air and Water mix to form the fog of possibility." Now raise both hands together to your heart level, and say, "All around me," while extending your hands outward to form a cross. [The visualization should be similar to that of the "Qabalistic Cross."]

3) Move to the easternmost point of the circle, face the east and say, "In the name of RAPHAEL [vibrate], I now banish air." Then, still holding the dagger in your right hand, make the Active Banishing Pentagram of Equilibrium [As in figure 8] while vibrating EHIEH. Then make the signs of the Portal [as in figure 6] by extending your hands in front of you palms outward, and then separating them as if opening a curtain or "veil." Then bring them together, as if allowing the veil to close. Then let your hands fall back to your sides.

4) Over top of the first pentagram, make the Banishing Pentagram of Air, while vibrating YEHUWAU. Then make the sign of the God Shu supporting the sky. Stand

with heels together, feet at ninety-degree angle, looking straight ahead. Both arms should extend outward horizontally, both elbows at ninety-degree angles, with forearms pointing upward. Both palms upward, as if holding up the sky.

5) Then thrust the dagger into the center of the pentagrams with both hands. At this point, you should feel the warm and moist air being forced out of the circle, past you from behind and out through the pentagrams in front of you.

6) After the flow of air stops, then move to the southernmost point of the circle, face the south and say, "In the name of MICHAEL, I now banish fire." Then make the Active Banishing Pentagram of Equilibrium once again, while vibrating EHIEH. Then make the signs of the Portal.

7) Over top of that pentagram, make the Banishing Pentagram of Fire, while vibrating ELOHIM. Then make the sign of the Goddess Thoum-aesh-neith. Stand with heels together, feet at ninety-degree angle, looking straight ahead. Both arms should bend at elbow, with both hands meeting at forehead. Thumbs at bottom and touching, fingers together, pointing upward to form a triangle with apex at top. Both index fingers should touch at tips.

8) Then thrust dagger into the center of the pentagrams, as in the last step. Now you should feel the hot and dry fire being forced out of the circle, past you from behind, and out through the pentagrams in front of you.

9) After the flow of fire stops, move to the westernmost point of the circle, face the west and say, "In the name of GABRIEL, I now banish water." Then make the Passive Banishing Pentagram of Equilibrium, while vibrating AGLA. Then make the signs of the Portal.

10) Over top of that pentagram, make the Banishing Pentagram of Water, while vibrating EL. Then make the sign of the Goddess Auramoth. Stand with heels together, feet at ninety-degree angle, looking straight ahead. Both arms should bend at elbows, with both hands meeting at navel level. Thumbs at top and touching, fingers together, pointing downward to form a triangle with apex at bottom. Both index fingers should touch at tips.

11) Then thrust the dagger into the center of the pentagrams, as before. You should feel the cold and wet water being forced out of the circle, past you from behind, and out through the pentagrams in front of you.

12) After the flow of water stops, move to the northernmost point of the circle, face the north and say, "In the name of AURIEL, I now banish earth." Then make the Passive Banishing Pentagram of Equilibrium once again, while vibrating AGLA. Once again, make the signs of the Portal.

13) Then over top of that pentagram, make the banishing pentagram of earth, while vibrating ADONAI. Then make the sign of the God Set fighting. Stand with right leg forward, right foot pointing front. Left leg should be behind right, with left foot perpendicular to right. Right arm should be extended upward and diagonally, palm facing front. Left arm should be extended downward diagonally, with palm facing back, and looking straight ahead.

14) Then thrust the dagger into the center of the pentagrams, as before. Now you should feel the cool and dry earth being forced out of the circle, past you from behind, and out through the pentagrams in front of you.

15) After the flow of earth stops, move back to the easternmost point of the circle, and touch the dagger to the center

of the pentagrams, which should still be in the east. This completes the casting of the circle.

16) Next you should raise the dagger on high, while circling back to the center of the circle, and then face the east.

17) With the dagger in both hands, fingers clasped and holding it at heart level, say, "and then, All is No-thing; Nothing But the pentagrams around the hexagram within Me."

18) Then vibrate "IYEHShTUAH ALOAH AYIN."

19) Now perform the Qabalistic Cross, as described in the Lesser Banishing Ritual of the Pentagram.

The Star Ruby

1) While standing in the center of the circle area, face the east and draw a deep breath. Holding the breath in, place your right forefinger against your lower lip. [This is the "Sign of Harpocrates or Silence," as illustrated in figure 10, on page 35. This will also be discussed in greater detail in chapter 8.]

2) Then move your right hand away with a great sweep back and out, expelling your breath while vibrating APO-PANTOS-KAKODAIMONOS.

3) Then with the right forefinger, touch your forehead and vibrate SOI. [The visualizations in these steps should be similar to the "Qabalistic Cross."]

4) Then move the right forefinger downward to the genitalia area, and vibrate OPHALLE.

5) Then move the right forefinger upward and across to your right shoulder, and vibrate ISCHUROS.

6) Then move the right forefinger across to the left shoulder, and vibrate EUCHARISTOS.

7) Then clasp both hands with fingers interlaced at abdomen level, and vibrate IAO.

8) Move to the easternmost point of the circle, face the east, and bending forward, imagine strongly an upright pentagram on your forehead. Draw both hands to eye level, grasp the pentagram by the sides, and thrust it forward. Leave your hands outstretched momentarily while leaning forward [This is the "Sign of Horus or The Enterer," as illustrated in figure 10. In addition, one should assume the God-

form of Horus while making this sign, as described in Appendix B. This will also be discussed further in chapter 12.] and vibrate THERION very loudly.

9) Then move to the northernmost point of the circle, face the north, and repeat Step 8, except vibrate NUIT [not too loudly].

10) Then move to the westernmost point of the circle, and repeat Step 8, except vibrate BABALON quietly.

11) Then move to the southernmost point of the circle, repeat once again, except vibrate HADIT loudly.

12) Then move to the easternmost point, completing the circle.

13) Step back to the center of the circle area, and face the east.

14) Perform the "Signs of N.O.X.":

A. (Puella) Facing the east, stand with your head bowed down, with your right arm across your breast and your left hand covering genital area. Then vibrate IO PAN.

B. (Puer) Facing the south, stand with your right arm extended outward horizontally, the elbow bent at a ninety-degree angle, with forearm pointing upward, palm facing forward. The left hand should be in a fist, thumb extended outward in front of the genital area. Then vibrate IO PAN.

C. (Mulier) Facing the west, stand with legs spread wide, extending arms outward. Then vibrate IO PAN.

D. (Vir) Facing the north, stand slightly bent forward, make both hands into fists, place them at your temples, with thumbs extended out to the sides. Once again, vibrate IO PAN. (See figure 7 for examples of Puer, Vir, Puella, and Mulier.)

15) Then face the east, extend both arms to the sides in the form of a cross, and say: PRO MOU IUGGES OPICHO MOU TELETARCHAI EPI DEXIA CHUNOCHES EPARIS-TERA DAIMONOS PHET EL GAR PERI MOU O ASTER TON PENTE KAI EN TEI STELEI O ASTEP TON EX ESTECHE. [This is a Greek version of the dialogue in Step 7 of the Lesser Banishing Ritual of the Pentagram.]

16) Repeat Steps 1 through 7.

CHAPTER 5

MEDITATION

To put it simply, meditation is the silencing of that inner voice that is almost constantly rambling on in a person's head. That is not as easy as it sounds, as anybody who meditates will tell you. The first few weeks of trying to meditate can be a frustrating period; but it is necessary to learn how to meditate effectively before beginning the practice of serious ritual. This chapter will lead into a step-by-step lesson in a form of meditation that will help prepare you to practice ritual magic.

When first learning how to meditate, you will find that your body attempts to reject the idea, by sending different messages to the brain. These messages may be telling you to scratch an itch, to shift your body weight, or possibly to rub a muscle cramp. In order to meditate effectively, you must force yourself to ignore these distractions.[1] Any itch will go away, the need to shift weight will subside, etc. You must apply considerable effort to remain focused on properly performing the meditation. If you have already successfully practiced other forms of yoga[2] or "transcendental" meditation effectively, then this exercise may be too basic or insufficient; however the beginner will find this exercise extremely adequate.

1) It is helpful to take a shower or bath before meditation. Water has a purifying effect on the body, besides being relaxing in general. Also, do not eat for several hours before meditation.

---

[1]Excluding severe muscle cramps, of course.
[2]See Appendix D.

2) It is also helpful to wear very little or no clothing; but if you feel uncomfortable, by all means wear something.

3) Find a quiet and dimly lit area where you won't be disturbed. If necessary, take the phone off the hook, and put up a "Do Not Disturb" sign.

4) Use no incense and burn no candles during this meditation.

5) Perform a banishing ritual.

6) It's interesting to note different effects while meditating facing a certain direction, but until you become adept at this exercise, it is best to face east.

7) Sitting on a chair or pillows on the ground is ideal. Meditating in different positions,[3] such as the Dragon, God or Lotus[4] may tend to produce different effects.

8) Start to control your breathing, taking long deep breaths. Inhale through your nose and exhale through your mouth. Concentrate on slowing down your breathing for a few moments. Pace your breaths. Very slowly begin to inhale, attempting to take up to 10 seconds while inhaling, and about the same exhaling. This may be difficult at first, so do the best you can.

9) Take five or six long deep breaths before closing your eyes. Continue breathing in this manner, but do not make a concentrated effort. Allow yourself to do it naturally. Then close your eyes and imagine yourself alone, enveloped in complete blackness and emptiness.

---

[3] Or "asanas." See Appendix D.
[4] See figure 12.

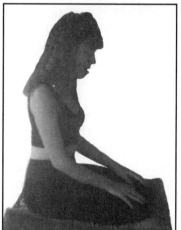

Figure 12. Yoga Positions. Top: The God; Bottom left: The Dragon; Bottom Right: The Lotus.

[Note: This next step may be difficult, possibly requiring several attempts to master. Just remember that persistence will pay off. Like any exercise, it gets easier each time that you try it.]

10) Now try to "empty" your mind. Release every thought that is in your mind. Let all be clear and black. Do not concentrate on stopping your thoughts. Allow them to enter your mind, and then tell yourself that you'll think about it later! Then allow the thought to leave for now. Try not to let yourself think about anything, without actually concentrating on "not thinking." This takes time at first, but gets easier with each attempt. It is hard to control your thoughts when you've never tried before. Beginners at meditation should be happy to experience a couple of minutes of "emptiness" while meditating, during the first month or two.

11) Continue in this manner for however long, until you can experience approximately 15 minutes of pure emptiness while meditating.

[Note: People who are experienced at meditating may be able to do this immediately, or within only a week or two. Being able to keep your mind completely clear is the first step in being able to control what normally controls you. It's a method of shutting off that voice that constantly rambles on in your head, the same voice that is reading these words at this very moment. It's not as easy as it sounds!]

12) After you become adept at clearing all thoughts from your mind during meditation, consider the following technique: Allow your mind to be completely clear for several minutes. Then realize the fact that you are not a human body at all, but a radiating orb or cloud of energy floating in empty space, with no limbs or flesh and blood. All is blackness and emptiness around you. No ground below, nor sky above. No up or down or direction. You should

become disoriented at first, which will disrupt your meditation. But continue trying, and you will become successful in experiencing something similar to free fall or zero gravity. You might consider yourself to be moving in a similar fashion as a planet moves around its sun. Rotating itself while orbiting its center point. There are many possible descriptions, all depending on the individual outlook.

[Note: Still do not allow any vocal or visual thoughts to enter your mind. Keep all black around you until you are able to enjoy the movement without any dizziness or disorientation.]

13) After you master the technique described in the last step, and can maintain that state for 15 minutes without difficulty, then move on to this step: Do not allow any audio or vocal thoughts into your mind, but allow yourself to experience any visual effects (such as flashes, colors or shapes) that present themselves to you. Do not create anything, or try to see anything. Just allow yourself to see whatever may appear before you.

[Note: Actual visions are probably astral, and considered undesirable during meditation.]

14) Do not concentrate on remembering everything during your meditation. You will remember anything that you need to, and then record your experiences immediately after meditating.

[Note: Allowing yourself to "hear" voices or sounds during meditation is not recommended, due to the distraction that they will cause. Voices also tend to affect you more directly. So unless the voice is overpowering, do not allow it to enter your mind.

Chapter 6

PERSONAL ENERGY

After several months of getting in shape physically, reading the proper texts, practicing banishing rituals and meditating daily, you are prepared to move on to the next step toward the practice of ritual magick. You have conditioned your body physically, and are beginning to strengthen your "personal energy." The next step is to conquer the astral plane.

Every living being is surrounded by a field of energy which is commonly called the aura. This energy animates the body it encompasses. Actually, it could be said that the aura immerses the body, as its energy permeates every tissue and cell.

Most theories suggest that the aura is generated by many power sources within the body that are called "chakras." The word "chakra" is derived from the Sanskrit[1] word "chakram," which means "a wheel" or "revolving disc." There are seven major chakras which are located in the general areas of the top of the head, forehead, neck, sternum, solar plexus, navel and genitalia. Hindu priests have been aware of this energy source, and have practiced building auric energy for many generations. They have given the chakras names, as noted in figure 13 on page 60.

There are numerous other minor chakras located all over the body, most notably at the palms of the hand and soles of the feet. Some theories suggest that the energy generates along the spine area, encircling the body above, below, and around the sides to meet in the front of the body.

---

[1]An ancient Indo-European language.

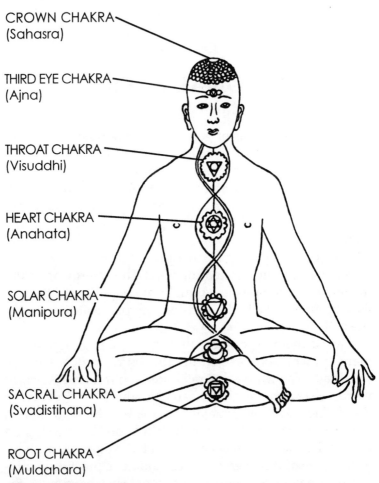

CROWN CHAKRA
(Sahasra)

THIRD EYE CHAKRA
(Ajna)

THROAT CHAKRA
(Visuddhi)

HEART CHAKRA
(Anahata)

SOLAR CHAKRA
(Manipura)

SACRAL CHAKRA
(Svadistihana)

ROOT CHAKRA
(Muldahara)

Figure 13. The Seven Chakras.

The energy is then absorbed by the body and repeats the cycle. It must be in constant motion in order to exist.

Every person has a certain level of personal energy that can be rated or graded, according to its quality and/or quantity. We all begin our lives with a natural grade that basically depends on the "age" of what is known as our "eternal spirit." This may or may not be the kind of age that we think in terms of, specifically measurements in "linear" time. You begin your "life" at "birth" and your level of energy may increase or decrease depending on your present and previous incarnations; but like an object in motion, you would tend to increase in velocity or strength. Every person has a different grade that is unique, which is to say that no two grades are exactly the same. Two people may be equally strong, but each will have weaknesses and strengths in different areas. Perfection is strived for, but very rarely is it ever achieved!

There is a definite relationship between the level of personal energy and the intensity of the aura. This is because the aura is composed of your personal energy, and it is the driving force of the physical body. It provides the spark necessary to crank up the machinery that animates the human robot. It could be said that the physical body represents "form" and the aura represents the "force" of the human body.[2] Another outlook is the body is "matter" and the aura is "motion."[3] Physically, the molecules of the body are very dense, and they are bonded very closely together, while the molecules in the aura are thinly spread, and they create the impression of a lack of substance. Auric energy possesses many interesting qualities. To name just a few:

1) It is capable of being built up or developed by exercise and usage.

2) It is capable of being depleted or drained by neglect or by "psychic attack."

3) It is capable of changing its form to resemble any particular shape.

4) It is capable of imitating certain "forces" which might attract or repel other forms of energy.

---

[2] In animals and plants, too.
[3] The aura is always in constant motion.

To see auras requires a certain visual talent that any person is capable of developing by practice. You will discover that the development of this talent is of utmost importance in your astral workings.

Start by looking at your own hand. Stare (not too intensely) at your hand for a period of time, until you notice a faint glowing around its edges. You probably won't see it at first because it takes the eyes several minutes to focus on it.[4] Depending on your sensitivity, you will notice something. There are many different descriptions of the aura, which range from a glowing light to effects similar to the smoke of dry ice rising off of the body. Every person sees the aura somehow differently.

After you are able to discern your own aura, begin watching other people and try to see theirs. Note the differences in the auras of different people. Try to discern shades of color and intensities. Look for shady or patchy areas. You will notice that it is always easier to spot the well-developed aura.

Most people are barely aware, if not completely unaware of their aura, and pay little or no attention to its development. It then remains weak and impotent, unable to compete with the greater mass of the physical body which requires its energy for motion.[5] It remains "trapped" by a purely subconscious or involuntary action of the body, except in certain cases involving total relaxation, such as sleep. Something like a magnetic attraction exists between the body and aura which is due to the "positivity" of the body and the "negativity" of the aura. Normally, the sheer mass of the body overpowers the aura, keeping it selfishly attached or confined to its space. By increasing the quality and quantity of the energy of the aura, you can build enough force to "match" the form of the body allowing it to escape from its prison.

---

[4] It may help to squint your eyes a bit.
[5] Besides a number of other things.

There are several methods of improving or intensifying the energy of your aura. Here are a few ways of stimulating the energy, causing motion of your aura which attracts energy to its flow. You simultaneously add energy to your supply (quantity) and increase the activity of the aura (quality).

1) Allow yourself to "feel" the energy flowing over your skin, surrounding your body at all times. At first, you will become forgetful during your normal daily activities, but persist and you will become aware of your aura naturally. It is always there and has always been there. It is a part of your body, in a similar manner as an arm or leg, or perhaps, a better reference would be the largest organ of the human body, the skin.

2) Meditate daily, as outlined in chapter 5, or do other yoga exercises, as discussed in Appendix D.

3) Exercise regularly and use vitamins. If you don't believe that something so basic and simple helps you build power, try taking vitamins (if you don't already) regularly, and you will surely notice an increase in your level of energy.

4) Perform the rituals daily as outlined in chapter 4.

5) Take up an art-related hobby, such as writing poetry or music, painting, or learn to play a musical instrument. Science and study must be balanced out by expression of emotion (or art)!

Aleister Crowley describes the well-developed aura as "a soap bubble of razor steel, streaming with light from within,"[6] and as extreme as that may sound, it is what we are striving for.

---

[6]*Magick in Theory and Practice*, chapter 12, pp. 99–100.

The aura is said to be "the magickal mirror of the universe." Since it does surround your body, any vision that your mind receives from your eyes has passed through your aura, and has been somehow affected by it. It's even possible that it is somehow involved in those cases of loss of memory pertaining to upsetting events in a person's life.[7] Also every other person sees you through your aura which affects their impression of you. When well-developed, your aura will hide your weaknesses and accent your strengths to provide different "faces" to the people with whom you have different relationships.[8] It is your protective shield from the rest of the universe and any dangerous—or even just irritating—influences that may decide to affect you. As with your physical body, take good care of your aura, and it will take good care of you.

---

[7]Such as car accidents and senseless acts of violence.

[8]One may be sweet and sensitive to one's lover, but they may show themselves differently to someone who cuts them off in traffic.

Chapter 7

UNIVERSAL STRUCTURE
AND THE ASTRAL PLANE

The presence of alternate planes—or dimensions—is a subject rarely discussed by modern theorists. Even today, in the space age, the majority of the world's population still refuses to acknowledge the reality of anything that cannot be seen or touched. In the many thousands of years that we have roamed Earth, it took until the late 1500's before the fact that the world is round was accepted socially. Additionally, it was only a mere thirty years ago that we finally managed to break free from Earth's gravitational pull, and walk on the Moon. That would have been considered an absurd suggestion just sixty years ago. It may take a few years longer before people will even consider the possibility of alternate planes of existence. However, I expect you to consider the following theories in all objectivity. These theories may help you understand the structure of the universe in which we live. This includes not only the physical universe that we see, but also a universe that most people are not even aware of, or could have any comprehension of. Those of us that choose to experiment with astral projection must be aware of its basic design, so that we may travel knowingly over that part known as the astral plane.

The basic structure of the universe as we perceive it, is in a network of planes or sections. There are four major sections that we recognize and describe as layers. In order to understand this structure we describe the four major planes as concentric circles in the names of the four basic elements. To be more specific, the center circle describes the earth plane, the circle around the center circle is the water plane, the third circle represents the plane of air and the outer circle defines the plane of fire. (See figure 14 below.)

In the center of figure 14 is the central core of Earth, or what is known as the terran plane. This is the area that our physical body is restricted to. This plane may also be described as the world of physical action. Ceremonial magicians refer to this zone as the world of manifestation. Earth matter is dense and unyielding, as is the physical body, itself. Every object existing on this plane is stable and solid, which makes them very difficult to change or transform.

As Earth is two thirds covered by water, that is the next plane above and around the core of Earth. The plane represented by the element water is the astral plane. This zone is nearest to the terran plane, and in part, is said to immerse much of the Earth plane. It can also be referred to as the zone of subtle action. Ceremonial magicians describe the astral world as that of formation. Every object in the astral world is made up of a more subtle composition, or what was described in chapter 6 as auric energy. Astral matter is much more easily affected and altered with the proper

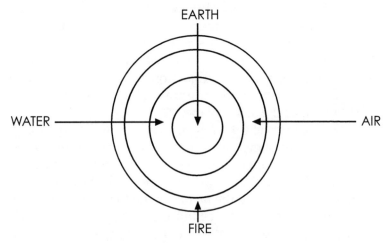

Figure 14. Basic Structure of the Universe: The Four Major Elemental Planes.

knowledge and understanding of its attributes, but it is also an elusive and evasive force to restrict.

The third layer is represented by the zone of air surrounding the worlds of water and earth. This is symbolically described as lots of empty space and very little activity, but in reality therein exists multitudes of life unperceived. This zone is termed as the etheric or spiritual plane.[1] This is referred to as the world of creation by ceremonial magicians. This plane is not actually relevant to astral work, except in the most advanced experiments; so we need not dwell on this subject, except to say that its outer border is on what is known as the "great abyss," which separates us from the celestial plane which shall be discussed next.

The fourth zone is the plane of fire and is referred to as the firmament or celestial plane. It is represented by the original source of fire and the actual core of the planetary universe, better known as Sol or the sun. The open and infinite space of the universe symbolizes the abyss separating humanity from divinity, and is constantly bathed in the light of the fiery sun, as are the worlds of air, water and earth. There are no possible descriptions of the celestial plane, because of the obvious difficulty in getting anywhere near it, due to the sheer power and force. Anyone who did reach this zone would be literally dissolved into its energy, and any hopes of return would appear pretty bleak. Ceremonial magicians refer to this plane as the archetypal world or world of emanations, and to eventually reach this plane is the long-term goal of every red-blooded magician.

This scenario represents much more than the structure of the physical universe we easily perceive. It is also a fairly accurate description of the dimensional universe as well. Most people do not relate to that area because normal human senses don't recognize it,[2] but as with forces such as magnetism and electricity, it is there nonetheless.

---

[1] This contradicts other popular theories held by popular occultists.
[2] Without specific training, which very few are willing to undergo.

Knowing the theory of the four major planes as described in this chapter, we move to examine specifically the astral plane. Each of the four planes may be subdivided into sections or subplanes. The terran plane is divided into four elemental subplanes in a similar fashion as the universe, as previously described. These four areas relate to the physical world in which we dwell usually.

The astral plane, however, may be divided into seven subplanes. The astral world and the terran plane interact with each other and in part, coexist in essentially the same space. In fact, any object existing on the terran plane has a corresponding shadow in the astral plane, much like the human aura. The area of the astral plane which encompasses the terran plane is termed the terran subplane of the astral. This is the zone occupied by the human aura in its usual state. It is also occasionally exposed to human eyes. Every so often, astral creatures or specters are glimpsed by some unsuspecting human in their normal activities. Also, people who have developed the art of seeing auras possess the ability to discern astral shadows, as the aura basically is; but in any case, the terran subplane of the astral is that part of the astral plane that shares the space of the terran plane, which is the surface of the planet we walk upon.

Four of the astral subplanes correspond with the four subplanes of the terran plane, and are also referred to by the basic elemental names of fire, air, water, and earth.

The astral world not only interacts with the terran plane, but also extends around and beyond the terran plane in a manner as described by two concentric circles. (See figure 15 on page 69.)

As the center core of Earth or the terran plane is divided into four worlds, so is the astral along with it.[3] (See figure 16 on page 70.) To illustrate this theory, con-

---

[3]Here again, the advanced student may disagree with these theories, but I would like to reiterate that this explanation is directed toward novice practitioners, in the hope of enabling them to grasp a difficult concept. To attempt an accurate description of the actual "positioning" of these dimensional planes will surely confuse the uninitiated.

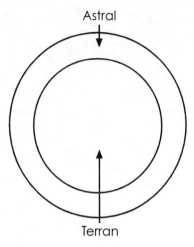

Figure 15. The Astral and Terran Planes.

sider your body to represent the center of the universe, symbolized by the very center of the X in figure 16. Wherever you stand, the universe surrounds you. Encircling your body are the four elemental subplanes, and they are in constant motion around you. But as you spin with the planet which is orbiting within the solar system (makes you kind of dizzy, doesn't it?), it can be very difficult to determine which direction you are actually facing (in relation to the universe). So science has conveniently devised the method of determining direction (in relation to the planet) utilizing the words north, south, east, and west. To make use of this directional system, we place the four elemental worlds in the four directions. The world of fire is placed in the south, air in the east, water in the west and earth in the north.[4]

---

[4]This directional system is accurate on the terran plane; but due to different "physical" laws being in effect on the astral plane, something like a mirror image of the terran transposes on the astral, which alters the directions of the elemental worlds of the astral (i.e., on the astral, the world of fire lies in the east, air in the west, water in the north and earth in the south. However, this is advanced and probably confusing, and is not pertinent at this point. Just keep in mind that on the terran plane, the worlds are as named above.)

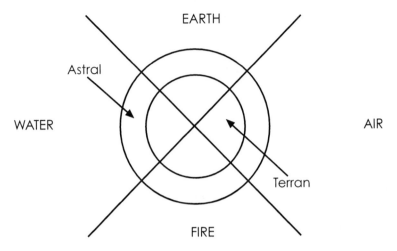

Figure 16. The Astral and Terran Planes Divided by the Elemental Subplanes.

The conditions of these elemental subplanes correspond to certain states. To human senses, the world of fire is hot and dry: a very desert like subplane of the astral. The world of air is warm and moist: a very humid and foggy or cloudy subplane of the astral. The world of water is cool and wet: a seemingly underwater subplane of the astral. The world of earth is cold and dry: an artic-like atmosphere and mountainous subplane of the astral.

There are also said to be dominant or prevalent astral creatures existing in each of the elemental subplanes. In the world of fire are salamanders, in air are sylphs (a very effeminate and dainty air being, seemingly angelic), in water are undines (a nymph or feminine water spirit, which according to legend, may obtain a human soul if one marries a human) and in the world of earth are gnomes. There are numerous other individual characteristics of each elemental subplane which are outlined in Table 2 on page 71. These should be studied to use as "landmarks" while traversing the astral plane. The table lists characteristics and dominant features of each of the elemental subplanes of the

Table 2. Characteristics of the Four Elements.

ELEMENTAL WORLD	FIRE	AIR	WATER	EARTH
Direction	South	East	West	North
Atmospheric conditions	Hot and dry, thin atmosphere	Warm and moist, humid atmosphere	Cool and wet, liquid-like atmosphere	Cold and dry, dense atmosphere
"Weather" conditions	Summerlike, dry heat	Cloudy, windy	Turbulent currents	Winterlike, cool and clear
Common landscapes	Desertlike, blazing sun, various oases	Skylines, fog	Beaches, rainforests, swampy areas	Mountainous, woods, dense foliage
Dominant coloring	Reds, oranges, deep yellows	Light yellows, light blues	Deep blues, deep greens	Light greens, browns, black
Dominant creatures	Salamanders, crawling creatures, reptiles, etc.	Sylphs, avians, butterflies,	Undines, also fish, porpoise, lobsters, etc.	Gnomes, also cats, dogs, elephants, etc.
Dominant foliage	Cactus, palms	Little foliage, some vines	Water lilies, reeds	Many varieties, oaks, pines, flowers, etc.
Likely odors	Cedar, tobacco	Musk, Mints	Salty air, jasmine	Fruity, flowery, earthy smells
Ruling constellations	Aries, Leo, Sagittarius	Aquarius, Gemini, Libra	Cancer, Scorpio, Capricorn	Virgo, Taurus, Pisces

astral plane. These correspondences may be helpful to the novice traveler in locating yourself, by recognizing the prominent landmarks and conditions which will be most commonly experienced in each of the elemental worlds.

Earlier, the dream subplane of the astral was briefly mentioned. This is also described as the world of illusion, although this does not always hold true. This plane should be termed as the world of possibility. It seems that many events occurring in this area prove to be warnings of some kind, either of good or bad things to come. Although many events that occur in dreams never take place, that is not to say that they wouldn't have happened, had circumstances been different; or if one had made a different decision at a turning point in one's life.[5]

Most theories on the dimensional planes suggest that the dream subplane exists between the terran and the astral worlds, and is usually described as a separate plane. The theory discussed here places the dream subplane of the astral below the terran subplane. It is suggested that while dreaming, one "falls" down to the dream subplane in an involuntary action of the astral body. This might possibly explain the common "falling" sensation experienced while dreaming, and may even shed some light on the expression "to fall asleep." Everyone who remembers their dreams is familiar with all of the possible settings, landscapes, and activities within the dream subplane, besides such things as weather conditions and wildlife. Additionally, many of us are aware that monsters do exist on this subplane.

The largest subplane of the astral is termed as the stratas, which ceremonial magicians refer to as the magickal plane. The stratas subplane is so large in fact, that it may be divided into several sub-subplanes in itself. Among its other aspects, this subplane interacts with the next major plane, that of air. That section of the stratas subplane that does interact with the world of air is termed the spiritual sub-subplane of the stratas subplane of the astral.[6] This zone is the highest section of the astral plane and the most difficult to reach. To do so would be a highly advanced exercise, besides being extremely disastrous to the uninitiated or novice, as the visions produced in this zone are inconceivable to all but a small handful of adept practitioners. In any

---

[5]Or even a small event, such as the simple decision to purchase a lottery ticket; although the chances of winning may be incredibly remote, this small action might cause your life to be permanently and drastically altered.

[6]This is partly because the world of air is termed the spiritual plane by magicians.

case, to rise to that level would take an incredible effort and unmeasurable skill, which is only attainable by years and years of daily practice and exercise. To accidently find yourself at this level would suggest an extremely high natural ability, and you should seek the training of a known and competent teacher of this art in order to sharpen and develop this obvious talent.[7]

There are numerous other sub-subplanes of the stratas subplane of the astral. These include what are called the tropical zone,[8] the nocturnal zone,[9] the sahara zone,[10] and "Symbolica."[11] There are numerous other sub-subplanes in the stratas subplane of the astral which need not be described here. You will have plenty of time to explore these areas soon enough. For descriptive purposes, the stratas subplane is positioned uppermost in the astral. Figures 17 and 18 (page 74) will give you an idea of the complete structure of the astral plane.

To conclude this chapter, it seems fitting to quote from *Magick in Theory and Practice* by Aleister Crowley:

> Every Magician possesses an Astral Universe peculiar to himself, just as no man's experience of

---

[7]Although teachers of astral projection or ritual magick are few and far between, such abilities seem to somehow attract the right teacher, but not necessarily. Use logic and judgment when accepting a teacher, because many are not what they claim to be. If a teacher tries to (proverbially) "baffle you with bullshit," or uses many overly technical terms which make little sense to you, it would probably be best to pass. Also, any unreasonable demand should be well considered. Do not allow a teacher to convince you to do anything that you do not want to do! If one threatens not to teach you unless . . . , then its best to say "OK, fine." There will be other teachers that will not want to use you for their own personal purposes. Do not compromise your principles for anybody.

[8]Which resembles a lush rain forest atmosphere with many exotic birdlike and small reptilian creatures, many watery areas and heavy underbrush.

[9]A very dark and starry night sky with heavy fog at "ground" level.

[10]Desertlike, with sands that change color according to "weather" conditions.

[11]Where often are seen plants, gardens, mountains and even creatures shaped in the form of particular symbols or hieroglyphics. Aleister Crowley and others term this subplane alchemical.

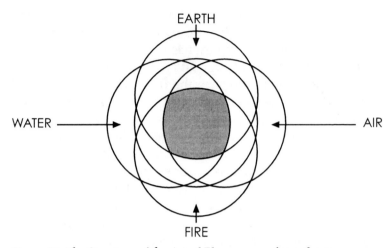

Figure 17. The Structure of the Astral Plane as seen from above.

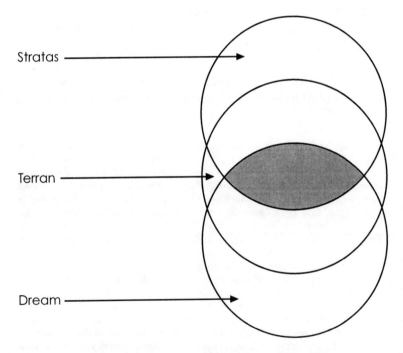

Figure 18. The Structure of the Astral Plane as seen from the side.

the world is conterminous with that of another. There will be a general agreement on the main points, of course; and so the Master Therion [Aleister Crowley] is able to describe the principle properties of these "planes," and their laws, just as he might write a geography giving an account of the Five Continents, the Oceans and Seas, the most notable mountains and rivers; he could not pretend to put forth the whole knowledge that any one peasant possesses in respect of his district. But, to the peasant, these petty details are precisely the most important items in his daily life. Likewise the Magician will be grateful to the Master Therion for the Compass that guides him at night, the Map that extends his comprehension of his country, and shows him how best he may travel afield, the advise as to Sandals and Staff that make surer his feet, and the Book that tells him how, splitting open his rocks with an Hammer, he may be master of their Virgin Gold. But he will understand that his own career on earth is his Kingdom, that even the Master Therion is no more than a fellow man in another valley, and that he must explore and exploit his own inheritance with his own eyes and hands.[12]

All symbolisms aside, Crowley is basically saying that the universe is a big place, and that what he may describe might not be what you see on your journeys (although it may, but that would be fairly unlikely). Map your astral plane, so you know where you have been and where you are going.

---

[12]Aleister Crowley, *Magick in Theory and Practice by The Master Therion* (Paris: LeCram Press, 1929; New York: Castle Books, n.d.), pp. 251–252.

Chapter 8

ASTRAL PROJECTION

People often confuse the aura with the "scin-laeca" or "astral body of light." The two are closely related, however there is a definite difference between them. The astral body is an extension of the aura. Some of the energy of the aura separates from the main supply into some form[1] away from the physical body.

It is safe to assume that since you can perceive your astral body, at least a part of your auric energy must remain within the physical body. While creating your astral body, you will experience a draining effect until you're able to transfer your consciousness to the astral body, which is still connected to your body by a "cord" or "chain of light," through which your energy flows. Your physical body will retain enough energy to maintain life, although breathing and heart rate will be greatly reduced. When you master the ability to transfer your consciousness to the astral body, then you will be equipped to travel on the astral planes. But first, it would be a good idea to "exercise" your aura with the methods described in chapter 6 for a period of at least a month and preferably longer, especially if you are a beginner. You must be able to fully distinguish the difference between your physical body and your aura.

It is commonly accepted that—whenever the astral body has been separated from the physical body—some connection must exist between them. In reality, the auric energy never actually divides into two completely separate bodies, for there is always a common link between the two.

---

[1]Any form that you may desire.

This link is sometimes referred to as the "silver cord" or "chain of light," and your personal energy flows along it while you are projecting astrally. Knowledge of this cord and its qualities can be quite useful while traveling, as its presence has both advantages and disadvantages.

Some theorists suggest that the source of the chain of light is at one of the chakras, and that the particular chakra varies with different individuals. However, the cord of every person I have observed, including myself, seems to originate from the "sacral" chakra, located just below the navel. This is symbolically appropriate, as that is the same point of origin as the umbilical cord between mother and child. In any case, my experiences are not so extensive as to deny the possibility that the cord may originate (or may appear to originate) from another point in some people.

For the beginner, astral vision will most probably be dim at best, and due to relatively adolescent or undeveloped energy, the cord will appear thin (or may not even be visible to the barely trained eye). Actually this is just as well, because it is best for the beginner to ignore its presence, as the cord's motion will tend to distract the novice.

Even though the cord is extremely thin and flexible, it is far from delicate, as many people believe. Some instructors of astral projection warn students to "be careful not to sever the silver cord, or you will not be able to return to the physical body, and will forever wander the astral plane as a specter of light." However, from personal observations and experimentation, I have found this to be completely untrue. The chain of light is, in fact, extremely difficult to sever, even when exerting considerable force. It acts much like fishing line on a spool. If a blow is delivered to the cord, it seems to simply move with the blow, seemingly pulling out more "line" from its source.

The fear of severing the cord is completely unfounded. One important point that supports this statement is the fact that dreaming is technically a form of astral projection, and that while dreaming we rarely, if ever, pay the slightest bit of attention to the silver cord, although theoretically, it remains ever-present. If ever the presence of the chain of light presents some problem, or does somehow become damaged, then it is suggested that you play it safe, and immediately return to the physical body. On your next experiment, your cord should be in perfect condition once again.

The astral body is sometimes referred to as the "body of desire." This is because you are able to shape this body into any form that you wish. One of the many practices of ceremonial magicians is the assumption of "God-forms." They study statues and pictures of a particular God, such as Osiris, Isis, or Apophis, and then form the astral body to resemble that God or Goddess.[2] This is an exercise used to exercise and strengthen control over the energy we possess, and to invoke more energy of a specific nature.[3]

Those of us that do indulge in the practice of assuming God-forms believe that by doing so we attract energy of a certain nature to our own energy, which mixes with and adds to our own personal supply. The nature of the energy corresponds to the attributes of the form we choose. For example, to assume the form of the Goddess Venus would attract love energy; to assume the form of Thoth would attract wisdom, etc.[4] In any case, this method of exercising the aura and body of light enhances the ability to work with astral forms by way of sheer practice.

As a useful example of this art, here shall be described the assumption of the God-form Harpocrates. He was also known as the younger Horus, and happened to be the son of the Egyptian deities Isis and Osiris, who were brother and sister.[5] Osiris was the first son of the union between the earth God Seb and the sky Goddess Nuit. Isis was their

---

[2]Also, see Appendix B.
[3]In relationship to the nature of the form we choose.
[4]I have greatly simplified this theory for basic explanatory purposes.
[5]It was all quite sordid, but perfectly legal in those days.

fourth child.[6] To assume the God form of Harpocrates, envision yourself to be approximately seven or eight feet tall, and larger in all areas. You should also envision a face and body of translucent emerald green, with blue eyes, blue hair, and a tall double crown of red and white. You should wear a collar of yellow and blue, a waistcloth of yellow and blue with a mauve girdle, and a lion's tail.[7]

This God-form should be assumed in conjunction with the "sign of silence," as described in chapter 4. You should stand with your feet six to eight inches apart, bend knees slightly, place the right hand at your side and inhale deeply. Then place your left hand's forefinger to your lips as if telling someone to hush.[8] Hold in the breath for several moments, and then release it, sweeping your left hand away from your body, while vibrating the name HARPOCRATES. Ceremonial magicians assume his form regularly to help build auric energy and, also, whenever returning to the physical body from any astral voyage or movement. To do this somehow insures complete restoration of the energy into the body. If you do not return to your physical body fully and in proper motion, your body suffers a kind of "whiplash" effect. The results can be dizziness, disorientation, possible headache and/or nausea, and occasionally even physical pain, like being slapped.

It may not be completely necessary to assume the form of Harpocrates upon "re-entry," but you should definitely slowly enter the space of your physical body and hold yourself in position while your body absorbs the energy of your astral body in its own time.[9] Never try to rush the reabsorbtion process, although most students do experiment to see how quickly they can return back into the body.

---

[6]Their second child was also named Horus, not to be confused with the younger Horus, child of Osiris and Isis, otherwise known as Harpocrates.

[7]Other God-forms are detailed in Appendix B.

[8]The "sign of silence" is performed with the right finger at the lips during the "Star Ruby," but normally you should use the left.

[9]At least several moments.

You can expect to miscalculate at least once or twice, and experience the discomfort, before realizing that it is much better to take your time, and do it properly.

All explanations as to why we possess the ability to project astrally would have to be either too technical to prove, or too abstract to believe. I have constructed the following explanation to help teach the subject, and although technically much remains unproven, it allows students to understand why it is a possible feat.

What a marvelous machine is the human body! Equipped with its many feet of tubing, pump, filters, quarts of fluid, valves, hinges, wires (nerves conduct electrical current), etc.; all enclosed within a latex-like fibrous material. It's quite an amazing system that depends on a series of coincidences to provide the proper conditions needed to animate it. I certainly can appreciate the intelligence needed to even understand how the body works, much less the technical genius capable of building one.

The ability to travel astrally is based on the idea that the physical body is merely a golem or flesh puppet controlled by some higher consciousness which is the "true self." This "true self" is possibly related to what is known as the "immortal spirit," "eternal soul," or the "holy ghost." This is the part of us that survives death and continues to some other incarnation. It is also the source of the logical voice that we hear in our heads and which is constantly advising us.

Now most people believe that the source of that voice is inside our heads. True, it is the point where we hear, see, and speak; but still, the contents of our skull does not include any control room with tiny beings running the helm of the human vessel. There is no computer talking to us from our brain. That mass of tissue and fluid does little more than control the movements of our limbs, regulates our breathing and heart rate, controls the release of certain hormones and chemicals, etc. Science tells us that the brain is also responsible for many other functions, such as intelligence, decision, memory, and even awareness; but how can this be conclusively determined? Nothing existing within our heads can be proven to possess the ability of reason or logic. Who is to say that some outer force is not responsible for conscious personality? This force may possibly be enclosed or immersed within the physical body, using it as a shelter or house which provides some form of protection that the force feels necessary for its survival; or maybe it enables the intelligent force to make specific actions in the physical world, which it would not be able to do in its pure energy form. In other words, it utilizes the human robot to perform specific tasks in this world. Ceremonial magicians believe that we all have one major act that must be performed in this world in order to progress in our spiritual attainment. This task is called the "Great Work."

There is an age-old belief that every soul was placed on Earth to fulfil some deed or perform some act, and that it is their part of the human machine to complete. Ultimately, this is the proverbial "meaning of life." Every individual's "meaning of life" is different and supposedly, as the soul progresses through its incarnations, we are given more difficult tasks to accomplish. Very few people in the world are able to realize the true meaning of their lives, much less to fulfill that act with time to spare. Those that do are considered to have a high degree of spiritual "enlightenment." In many cases, people tend to look forward to future death, so that they might progress in spiritual attainment. This may sound self-destructive, but in reality, it is quite the opposite. They are anxiously anticipating their next "Great Work."

CHAPTER 9

ASTRAL EXERCISES

Chances for success in practicing the art of astral projection are dependant on your development of your aura,[1] and on your talent to "see" auras or auric energy. By following the procedures listed in previous chapters[2] for a period of several weeks, you should have (at least) begun to improve your aura, and increase personal energy.

The ability to work with personal astral energy is based on your capability to detect auric energy. In other words, you must first develop the technique of "seeing" human auras and for that matter, the aura of any object, with your physical eyes before it is possible for you to work with said energy.

Who knows where the images we perceive through our eyes are transmitted? If you accept the theory discussed earlier,[3] you would have to realize that the human eye is nothing more than a remote control camera that relays a signal to the "self." In any case, you can safely assume that while traveling astrally, you do not see things through your physical eyes. Your astral visions are perceived by what is known as the "Third Eye."

The chakra located at the forehead is said to house the organ of vision of the aura. As described in chapter 6 on personal energy, the chakras are the "energy sources" of the human aura, and there are seven major chakras located

---

[1]Which will accordingly increase the level or grade of personal energy.
[2]Such as the meditation outlined in chapter 5, the methods of developing the aura and the practice of discerning auras, as described in chapter 6.
[3]Pertaining to the human body as being merely a robot controlled by some higher force, termed as the "true self."

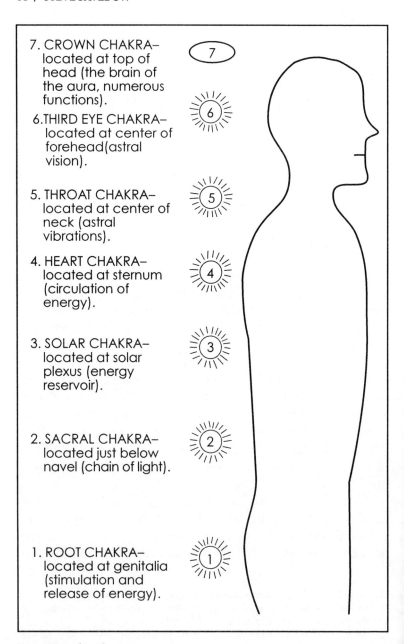

7. CROWN CHAKRA–ocated at top of head (the brain of the aura, numerous functions).

6. THIRD EYE CHAKRA–located at center of forehead(astral vision).

5. THROAT CHAKRA–located at center of neck (astral vibrations).

4. HEART CHAKRA–located at sternum (circulation of energy).

3. SOLAR CHAKRA–located at solar plexus (energy reservoir).

2. SACRAL CHAKRA–located just below navel (chain of light).

1. ROOT CHAKRA–located at genitalia (stimulation and release of energy).

Figure 19. The Chakras.

within the body. Each chakra also represents, composes, or encloses an astral organ of the aura. Each organ is responsible for some vital function of the aura, as illustrated in figure 19.

As previously stated, the chakra located at the forehead houses the "Third eye," the organ of vision in the astral body. Through your ability to see astral shapes, you may form shapes utilizing your own supply of personal energy. In actuality, you create some form with your mind or self, as that is the receptor of the images you perceive. To be more specific, by willing your "self" to see some object, it then creates that object for you to see. In a sense, you mold your auric energy with your mind, much like a sculptor would do with a lump of clay. This may sound abstract, but by practicing the following five astral exercises, you can conquer the art of astral projection. Work at the first exercise until you achieve successful results, and then master each individually before moving on to the next.

Astral Exercise 1
Initial Separation

The first step in astral projection is the formation of a body in which to travel across the astral plane. The following exercise is the proper method of creating that astral body. The first step in any venture is the most difficult, and astral projection is most definitely no exception. This first exercise alone may take many attempts before you notice any definite results. Don't become discouraged with the small failures, for you are capable of successfully mastering this procedure in your own time. Be persistent!

1) Begin as in the meditation outlined in chapter 5. Do not eat for several hours beforehand. Taking a bath or shower, and wearing little or no clothes can be helpful practices to start.

2) Work in a quiet, dimly lit, or dark room where you won't be disturbed. If necessary, put up a "Do not disturb" sign and take the phone off the hook.

3) Do not use candles or incense with this exercise.

4) Perform a banishing ritual.

5) Sit in a chair or on cushions on the floor in the center of your working area and face east. It is best to keep your back vertical. Note: Many people do work best while laying on their back; but for the beginner, it's best to sit up with your back straight.

6) Begin as you would the meditation exercise. Start to control your breathing, taking long, slow, deep breaths. Inhale through your nose and exhale through your mouth. Concentrate on slowing down your breathing for a few moments. Pace your breaths. Start to inhale very slowly, taking up to ten seconds while inhaling, and about the same exhaling.

7) Take five or six long deep breaths before closing your eyes. Continue breathing in this manner without actually making a concentrated effort to. Allow yourself to breathe this way naturally. Imagine yourself alone, enveloped in blackness and emptiness before attempting to clear all thoughts from your mind as described in the meditation exercise.

8) As you empty all thoughts from your mind, become extremely aware of your aura as it flows over your body. Feel it wrapping around your torso and limbs, much like a wind or breeze blowing across your skin.

9) In the emptiness of your mind, picture your body sitting in its place, surrounded by a luminescent cloud or form

of energy of a similar size and shape as the physical body. This energy is radiating a white or crystalline glow just past the boundaries of the body. Know in your mind that this cloud of energy is your "self."

10) Concentrate on your "self" as this body of energy, knowing that it is a separate entity from your physical body and free of its restrictions.

11) This step may take many attempts before mastering. You must picture your "self" directly in front of you as if you were looking into a mirror. See your own body sitting before you.

Note: Of course, your physical eyes remain closed. You must see this body through your "mind's eye" or "third eye." Most people have difficulty at first with sight through the third eye. It is hidden and protected by the chakra surrounding it, which acts as kind of an eyelid. The third eye may remain weak and undeveloped due to lack of usage, although development of the aura as a whole will strengthen its vision, as well as improve the workings of all the astral "organs."

12) Place the thought in your mind that there is another body sitting directly in front of you and "see" it there. Do not think to yourself, "This is just my imagination." Know for a fact that your body is directly in front of you, and then examine it without moving from the place where you are sitting. Note general details such as hair, facial features, and body shape. See that it is you! Your vision will probably be fuzzy and the body may only appear as a faint shadow for some time. Do not try to see a clear picture at first. Let it come to you as it will. Make out any details that you can without actually forcing yourself to see any details very closely.

Note: On the first several attempts of this exercise, remain positioned in front of your "self" as if looking into a mirror.

At the point where you can clearly picture your "self" before you, then you are within your astral body and are in actuality, looking at your physical body. You have transferred your consciousness to the body of energy which you have created outside of your own physical body. It may take weeks of steady practice (attempted at least once daily) before your astral vision provides a clear picture of yourself; so take your time and become adept at this exercise, as it is the foundation for all of your astral workings. The twelve previous steps are the proper procedure for beginning any astral journey, as these next steps are the proper procedure for returning to the physical body.

13) While facing the body, sit and assume the same position that the body is in. Move yourself closer to examine the features and details of the face until you are virtually nose to nose with it.

14) Then try to squeeze against it as if giving it a hug, trying to feel the solidity of it. This should all be done very slowly and deliberately, as if moving in slow motion.

15) After you have pushed your way into the body, slowly move to assume the same position as the body, facing the same direction. Then hold yourself in place for several moments. See that there is nothing but empty space in front of you. All should be black and emptiness.

16) After several moments, assume the God-form of Harpocrates, as described in chapter 8.

17) Perform a banishing ritual.

18) Record all experiences, events, sensations, etc., in your magickal records.

The importance of proper restoration of your auric energy into the body cannot be overemphasized. Most people have little or no excess personal energy to spare. The human body is a very balanced and sensitive device which requires a specific amount of energy to operate properly. In the majority of cases, one possesses minimal energy levels at best and consequently, the loss of even a small amount of personal energy could conceivably result in a variety of unpleasant conditions. Depending on the individual, one might experience effects ranging from dizziness and headaches, to anxiety and schizophrenia, in the worst cases.

Remember not to rush the re-absorbtion process. No matter how successful the astral separation may be, it is most important that you make a concentrated effort to properly restore your energy to the body. The chances are that most people will experience some kind of discomfort from inadequate "re-entry" at least once. In mild cases of discomfort, many times drinking a glass of cold water, or taking a relaxing bath, will be most helpful. Sometimes it is necessary to "sleep it off." Your body will naturally, although slowly, attract the needed energy by itself in time. In more severe cases, it is sometimes necessary to attempt to retrace your astral steps, and then return to your body once again, taking greater care to insure full restoration of your energy. It is believed that by doing this, you will retrieve whatever energy you may have lost.

By following Steps 13 through 16 of the previous exercise, you should adequately return your personal energy to the physical body. After a successful journey and proper restoration of energy, you would ideally feel refreshed and energetic, although this may not be the case until you become fairly adept at this, and the following exercises.

Astral Exercise 2
Developing Astral Senses

The development of the senses is essential to survival on any plane. If you have not managed to sharpen your physical senses over the years, then it might be quite a challenge to sharpen your astral senses.[4] Smell, vision, hearing, touch, and even taste are senses that will prove to be most helpful, if not necessary, while exploring the astral plane. The following exercise is basic in its tendency to sharpen and develop the senses of your astral body.

1) Before beginning this exercise (but after bathing and/or disrobing), place burning incense (traditionally jasmine or ginseng) in the east of your working area. Then place a lit candle in the south, a large glass of water in the west and a dish of salt in the north.

2) Perform a banishing ritual.

3) Stand where you will be working in the center of the room, facing east. Then slowly walk forward to the burning incense and smell its aroma for several moments.

4) After several moments, move around to the south in a circular motion to where the candle is burning and then gaze at its flame for several moments.

5) After several moments, move around to the west in a circular motion until you come to the glass of water, and then feel it with your hand for several moments.

6) After several moments, move to the north in a circular motion until you come to the dish of salt. Then touch it with your fingers, and taste it.

7) Now move once more in a circular motion to the east until you come back to the burning incense. Then turn,

---

[4]However, this is not to say that a deaf, blind or mute person wouldn't be able to travel. On the contrary, most people who are deprived completely of one sense, such as sight, will have strengthened their other senses almost involuntarily. In any case, a physically blind person, for example, would still theoretically be capable of perceiving astral vision.

move back to the center of the circle area and sit down, facing the east.

8) Next follow Steps 5 through 12 of Astral Exercise 1.

9) After you are able to discern your physical body in its position and are looking at it as if you were looking into a mirror, then turn your "back" to the physical body, and look away from it into the blackness.

[Note: Steps 10 through 14 that follow are rather difficult, and they may take many attempts to master. You should not dwell on any of these steps. If you do not succeed after several moments of trying, abandon the effort, and move to the next step. Keep moving through the procedure, and finish the whole exercise. These steps may take many weeks of frequent practice before obtaining successful results. Your senses will improve in proper time, which varies according to individual natural grade and talents.]

10) Attempt to move slowly forward to where the incense is positioned. Move by following the smell of the incense before you. You know it is there, because you can smell it burning; so move toward the smell, using it as a guide. You will soon come to the place where it is burning. Feel your "self" moving in a forward motion toward it. Locate the burning incense and then stop for several moments to smell it, as you did before beginning the exercise.

11) After several moments, attempt to move around to the south in a circular motion until you "see" the flame of the candle burning. This time, use the light of the flame to guide your movements. Move closer to the point where the candle is burning, and then stop to gaze at it for several moments.

12) After looking into the candle flame for several moments, move around to the west in a circular motion until you come

to the place where the cup of water is sitting. At this point, you must attempt to touch the water with your "astral hand."

13) Look down to where your hand should be, and concentrate your vision on the luminescent auric energy shaped in the form of a hand. This is your "astral hand."

14) Place the thought in your mind that you are putting your fingers into the glass of water. See your hand touching the water, and try to feel its cool wetness.

15) After you have succeeded in "feeling" the water for several moments, move around to the north in a circular motion until you come to the place where the dish of salt is sitting. At this point, you must attempt to use your astral hand once again to touch the salt with your fingers, and then try to "taste" it with your "astral mouth."

[Note: Your astral body is basically a duplicate of your physical body, complete with hands, legs, face, mouth, etc. You are using the past experience of tasting things with your mouth, and in a like manner, doing so in the same fashion on the astral.]

16) After tasting the salt for several moments, move around in a circular motion to the east until you are back to the point where the incense is burning. This completes the circle.

17) Standing before the burning incense, turn your back on it and move forward to where your physical body sits in the center of the room.

18) Then sit down in front of your body and imitate its position as if you were looking into a mirror. Sit as close as possible, facing the front of the body, and look closely at the facial features, slowly moving closer until you are virtually nose to nose.

19) At this point, push up against the body as if you were giving it a hug until you feel the solidity of its mass and form. Continue as in Steps 13 through 18 of Astral Exercise 1 (page 88).

It is advisable to ignore any other distractions that may present themselves to you while performing this exercise. Note all that you detect and record them afterward, but do not allow yourself to become distracted and wander away from your working area. Complete the exercise methodically, and then return to your body.

Astral Exercise 3
Astral Creation

Those involved in the art of astral projection often find it necessary to "create" astral objects for use in their journeys. To do this, you basically "utilize" some of your personal energy to create some object which may prove useful during your travels.

Much like the creation of your astral body, the ability to create an astral object is dependant on the ability and talent to "see" astral or auric energy. If you have successfully mastered the last two exercises, you should be able to easily discern auric energy through both your physical eyes and your third eye, or "mind's eye."

While exploring the astral plane, it would be most helpful, if not essential, for you to possess both a sword and dagger for your convenience and protection. If you do have a favorite dagger and/or sword, as most respectable magicians probably do, then it would be most appropriate to create imitations or duplicates of these weapons for your astral workings. The following exercise will describe exactly how you may create these weapons for your "self."

On your first few attempts of this exercise, it would prove helpful to follow Steps 1 through 12 of Astral Exercise 1 before beginning; however, after a couple of attempts, you will find that it is possible to practice this in almost any environment, for it is not actually necessary to leave the body during this particular exercise. Most people cannot detect astral energy or auric forms, even if it is directly under their nose, so there is no reason why this could not be practiced at one's job, or even in the line at the grocery store.

1) If not starting with Steps 1 through 12 of Astral Exercise 1, then begin by following Step 8 of Astral Exercise 1, by becoming extremely aware of your aura. Concentrate on it until its presence around your body becomes the primary thought in your mind. Feel it flowing over the skin of your body, wrapping around your torso and limbs in a constant motion, much like a breeze or breath of air surrounding you.

2) Keeping the presence of your aura foremost in your mind, look down at your hand, and concentrate your vision on the luminescent auric energy shaped in the form of a hand.

3) If remaining in the physical body while practicing this exercise, then try to separate your astral hand from your physical hand. Concentrate your vision on your astral hand, trying to remove the physical hand completely from vision, even though it may remain in the same space.

4) At this point, envision your dagger flowing outward from your astral hand, point first and followed by the blade, until the handle or hilt of the dagger is touching your fingers.

[Note: This will be quite difficult for beginners and it is almost never mastered during the first few attempts, except in the case of skilled practitioners. For many it is difficult to even determine success. It may take weeks of steady practice before the weapon becomes recognizable as such; but keep in mind that it is possible to practice this exercise almost anywhere.]

5) After obtaining satisfactory results creating the dagger (probably after several attempts), create your sword in the same manner as that described with the dagger.

6) If you have separated in order to perform this exercise, follow Steps 13 through 18 of Astral Exercise 1 (on page 88).

It is always considered wise to carry both a dagger and sword whenever traveling upon the astral plane for defensive purposes, among the many possible uses. Needless to say, you should also create sheaths for both weapons somewhere on your astral body, as you will need your hands to be free the majority of the time.

Your astral weapons should feel as "real" to you as any physical weapons would, although astral weapons will not obviously affect physical matter. Astral energy may pass right through physical objects, seemingly causing no effects. As a general rule, astral weapons will only affect astral matter. However, experienced practitioners will realize that astral energy does affect terran objects in subtle ways, with proper knowledge and understanding of the properties and natural laws of both.

Astral Exercise 4
Astral Manipulation

By practicing the three previous exercises, you should have begun to discover how to utilize your personal energy for creative purposes. There are certain advantages in mastering methods of manipulating auric energy to create astral forms, although at this point you probably do not see any actual benefits (other than possibly self-satisfaction) from these "small" efforts. After mastering this next exercise, it is believed that you will learn how to reap some material gain from the astral plane. This is a method of astrally creating a desired object, which (theoretically) should cause the manifestation of said object within the material world or terran plane.

There may be some "thing" that you desire, such as a radio, for example. Although it may not be difficult to form the shape of a radio utilizing your own personal energy, such as you did with the dagger and sword, it would prove pointless; for as the weapons created from astral energy are astral weapons, so the radio you would form is an astral radio. No matter how solid you may be able to form that radio, since there are no radio stations located anywhere on the astral plane (much less directed electrical energy as we know it), you would be very lucky to even pick up static on it.

There are however, methods of "finding" the astral form of a radio on the astral plane (specifically the terran subplane of the astral), which should cause it to find you on the terran plane. The following exercise is one effective procedure for doing so.

Before and during this exercise, you must establish a firm and clear "picture" of the desired radio (or whatever) in your mind, without actually creating it from your own personal energy.

1) Follow Steps 1 through 12 in Astral Exercise 1 (on page 85).

2) After separating from your physical body, create your astral sword and dagger as in Astral Exercise 3 (on page 93).

3) Sheath the sword and carry the dagger in your hand.

4) With the picture of the radio (or any desired object) fixed firmly in your mind, turn your back on the physical body (which should be sitting in its place), face east and

begin to move slowly in a circular motion to your right as if circling the physical body.

5) Slowly circle the body in a clockwise spiral, moving a little further away from it with each revolution or circumbulation. Doing this insures that your physical body will always remain directly to your right hand side. To return, all you would have to do is make a 90-degree turn to your right, and then move directly forward in order to return to where your physical body rests.

[Note: There are natural laws of attraction between your "self" and your body which involves the cord or chain of light described in chapter 8. It is the connection or link between the "self" and the body, and can help lead you back to the body when disoriented.]

6) As long as you manage to keep the desired object pictured firmly in your mind, you will run across that object sooner or later.

[Note: If you tire before finding the object, return to the body, as described in Step 5, then follow Steps 13 to 16 of Astral Exercise 1 in order to properly re-enter your body. You may then try again to find the object during your next practice session. This exercise, as with the others, will take several attempts to master.]

7) When you locate the desired astral form, you must next establish a link between it and yourself. The best way to do this is by taking your astral dagger, which you should be carrying in your hand, and plunging it into the desired object. Never do this to any seemingly "living" form such as a plant or animal, as this act will negatively affect the form, possibly irreparably.

[Note: Do not turn away from your path to circle the desired object. Always face the direction in which you were moving or remember to resume that direction after turning away.

8) Leave your dagger in the desired object and then unsheathe your sword. If you have been proceeding in the circular motion away from your physical body as you should have, and have not turned away from your path, then make a 90-degree turn to your right and walk forward with sword in hand, until you return to your body.

9) Assume the same position as your body, looking at it as if you were looking into a mirror. Then follow Steps 13 through 18 of Astral Exercise 1.

Feel free to create another dagger at the beginning of your next experiment. Your new dagger may be an exact duplicate of the original, or you might want to create a new design. Follow your own preferences. The first dagger will remain in the object where you placed it, until it is removed astrally.

Do not expect immediate results from this experiment. You have created a link between yourself and the desired object, however that is not to say that it will magickally appear before you instantly. It may take a bit of time, but you will find that object in its physical form some time in the near future. At that time, you may recover your astral dagger from the object of your desire.

Astral Exercise 5
Rising on the Planes

During the previous four astral exercises, our actions have been restricted to the terran subplane of the astral. This subplane is nearest to, and essentially a shadow of, the terran plane; however, it comprises only a small part of the astral plane, as described in chapter 7. There are many strange and alien places located away from the terran.

Many astral travelers are content to explore the terran subplane, as that is where material "things" dwell, and it is possible to obtain these "things" by affecting them from this subplane. On the other hand, there are those few people who are not driven by the religious symbol of our time—specifically the dollar sign—which represents the material luxuries available today. Consequently, people who seek to expand their universe find it necessary to move away from the material world in which we live. The best way to do that is by traveling straight up and away from the terran plane. The following exercise describes how to "Rise on the Planes," experiencing vertical motion on the astral plane.

It would be wise to practice each of the previous astral exercises until becoming adept at each individually, before attempting this exercise.

1) Begin by following Steps 1 through 12 of Astral Exercise 1.

2) At the point where you are sitting in front of your body as if looking into a mirror, create your astral sword as in Astral Exercise 3.

3) Raise your sword over your head with both hands, pointing it straight up into the sky.

4) Allow your astral body to "push" itself upward, holding the sword above you, as if it was lifting you away from ground level. Attempt to rise directly upward, and avoid veering to any one direction.

5) At "ground level," you should be surrounded by blackness. As you rise, allow yourself to see the coloring change to more of a dark blue, which should change to a dark purple as you continue to rise higher.

6) Continue to rise up as high as you possibly can go. Try not to take note of anything happening around you. Concentrate fully on rising upward. It may be easier to spiral upward, turning your astral body in a revolving manner. Be sure to rise directly vertically, without veering in any one direction.

7) At the point where you feel that you cannot possibly rise any higher, stop and examine the surroundings without moving from the place you have risen to. Look around and note the scenery and landscape. Ignore any living creatures that you may see. Note their presence, but do not interact with them.

8) After taking in all visions that may present themselves to you, begin to fall slowly downward. Follow the same direct path that you rose on. Descend toward the place from where you came. There should be a natural "pulling" sensation, which involves the connection between your astral and physical body. Try to check your falling, if you feel that you are moving too fast. Again, concentrate on your descension, rather than anything around you.

9) Eventually, you will return to your physical body. At that point, follow Steps 13 through 18 of Astral Exercise 1.

Advanced Astral Exercises

After successfully mastering these five astral exercises, you should naturally follow your own path of more and more difficult experiments on your own accord. There are a few suggestions, however, that may help relatively inexperienced students get started on the right foot.

After becoming adept at the previous exercise (probably after four or five attempts), begin to explore a bit in these "upper" areas. Remember to avoid interaction with other astral forms, until becoming familiar with the manuevering abilities of your astral body, and well experienced with the use of your astral weapons. Never trust human-like creatures until developing a friendly rapport, and even then remain ever cautious. Not all are malevolent, but enough are to warrant the use of extreme caution. If any astral creature should approach with the least bit of aggression, you should draw the banishing pentagram of water before them, while vibrating EL. This should disperse most astral creatures; but if it does not, try the banishing hexagram of water, while vibrating ARARITA.[5]

In fact, when any symbol is drawn in this manner, it will result in the stimulation of some specific reaction on the astral plane. It is recommended that you experiment extensively with each pentagram and hexagram illustrated in chapter 4, in the terran plane, as well as in each of the astral subplanes, and thoroughly document all data concerned in your magickal records. Also, it would be of immense value to experiment with all mystic symbols, including the cross, triangles, astrological sigils, Hebrew letters, swastikas, the unicursal hexagram, and the like.

The following astral exercises are also highly recommended.

1) The astral performance of "The Middle Pillar Ritual," and the different banishing rituals outlined in chapter 4, as well as the various rituals outlined in future chapters.

2) Many astral travelers find it advantageous to possess certain astral "tools" or "weapons" during their journeys.

---

[5]If neither of these seem effective, try the invoking pentagram of fire while vibrating ELOHIM. Otherwise, you would have to determine which specific element the creature represents, and use the banishing pentagram of that element, or the invoking pentagram of its opposite; i.e., water is opposite to fire, and earth is opposite to air.

These items may be created in the manner described in Astral Exercise 3.

A. The dagger and sword, which should have already been created to meet individual specifications.

B. The shield or disc should be round, approximately two or three feet in diameter, and is traditionally emblazoned with a hexagram on the front.

C. The staff or wand should be approximately four to five feet in length, and traditionally with seven knots, representing the seven major chakras, evenly spread along its length.

D. The helmet should cover the upper face down to eye level, and also down the sides of the face to conceal the main facial features. It should be lightweight and is traditionally of a yellow metal, such as gold.

Note: Weapons should only be used in a strictly defensive manner. They may be arranged to be carried on the astral body. The shield may be worn across the back, sheathes should be created to carry the dagger and sword, the staff may be carried, and the helmet, of course, may be worn. Whether or not these weapons are of utmost neccessity is questionable, although this exercise is of the highest value in perfecting the ability to create astral objects. Also, it is always worth the short delay it takes to create these tools, as they are often quite useful during one's travels. The magickal weapons will be discussed fully in chapter 11.)

3) It is always wise to create a refuge for yourself somewhere on the astral plane. It should be easily accessible to you, yet hidden from others. This may be a garden, a forest, a mountaintop, a house, or even on the moon. This may be done by picturing the place in your mind, and then walking away from your body, similar to the manner described in Astral Exercise 4; or by first rising up and away from the

physical body, and then circling as described, until finding the place.

4) The creation of an artificial elemental creature. Utilize your personal energy to create a living astral creature. If you prefer, it may resemble a cat or dog, or even a unicorn. Generally, it will take several attempts to create an actually animate creature, for it will tend to remain statuelike. A good idea, in this case, is to first create the creature during one experiment, and then return to your physical body. Afterward, return and attempt to animate it during your next experiment. Artificial elementals have been found to be excellent companions and guardians while traveling, for they are essentially an extension of yourself; and because they have been created from your own personal energy supply, these creatures will naturally tend to your well-being before their own.

Instructions for "Rising on the Planes"
BY ALEISTER CROWLEY[6]

1) Let the student be at rest in one of his prescribed positions, having bathed and robed with proper decorum. Let the place of working be free from all disturbance, and let the preliminary purifications, banishings and invocations be duly accomplished, and, lastly, let the incense be kindled.

2) Let him imagine his own figure (preferably robed in the proper magical garments, and armed with the proper magical weapons) as enveloping his physical body, or standing near to and in front of him.

---

[6]"Liber O vel Manus et Sagittae," from *Magickal Theory and Practice* (New York: Castle Books, n.d.), pp. 387–389.

3) Let him then transfer the seat of his consciousness to that imagined figure; so that it may seem to him that he is seeing with its eyes, and hearing with its ears.

This will usually be the great difficulty of the operation.

4) Let him then cause that imagined figure to rise in the air to a great height above the earth.

5) Let him then stop and look about him. (It is sometimes difficult to open the eyes.)

6) Probably he will see figures approaching him, or become conscious of a landscape.

Let him speak to such figures, and insist upon being answered, using the proper pentagrams and signs, as previously taught.

7) Let him travel at will, either with or without guidance from such figure or figures.

8) Let him further employ such special invocations as will cause to appear the particular places he may wish to visit.

9) Let him beware of the thousand subtle attacks and deceptions that he will experience, carefully testing the truth of all with whom he speaks.

Thus a hostile being may appear clothed with glory; the appropriate pentagram will in such a case cause him to shrivel or decay.

10) Practice will make the student infinitely wary in such matters.

11) It is usually quite easy to return to the body, but should any difficulty arise, practice (again) will make the imagination fertile. For example, one may create in thought a char-

iot of fire with white horses, and command the charioteer to drive earthwards.

It might be dangerous to go too far, or to stay too long; for fatigue must be avoided.

The danger spoken is that of fainting, or of obsession, or of loss of memory or other mental faculty.

12) Finally, let the student cause his imaginary body in which he supposes himself to have been travelling to coincide with the physical, tightening his muscles, drawing in his breath, and putting his forefinger to his lips. Then let him "awake" by a well-defined act of will, and soberly and accurately record his experiences.

It may be added that this apparently complicated experiment is perfectly easy to perform. It is best to learn by "travelling" with a person already experienced in the matter. Two or three experiments should suffice to render the student confident and even expert.

Crowley goes on to the next exercise:

1) The previous experiment has little value, and leads to few results of importance. But it is susceptible of a development which merges into a form of Dharana—concentration—and as such may lead to the very highest ends. The principal use of the practice in the last chapter is to familiarise the student with every kind of obstacle and every kind of delusion, so that he may be perfect master of every idea that may arise in his brain, to dismiss it, to transmute it, to cause it instantly to obey his will.

2) Let him then begin exactly as before, but with the most intense solemnity and determination.

3) Let him be very careful to cause his imaginary body to rise in a line exactly perpendicular to the earth's tangent at

the point where his physical body is situated (or to put it more simply, straight upwards).

4) Instead of stopping, let him continue to rise until fatigue almost overcomes him. If he should find that he has stopped without willing to do so, and that figures appear, let him at all costs rise above them.

Yea, though his very life tremble on his lips, let him force his way upward and onward!

5) Let him continue in this so long as the breath of life is in him. Whatever threatens, whatever allures, though it were Typhon and all his hosts loosed from the pit and leagued against him, though it were from the very Throne of God Himself that a voice issues bidding him stay and be content, let him struggle on, ever on.

6) At last there must come a moment when his whole being is swallowed up in fatigue, overwhelmed by its own inertia [This is in case of failure. The results of success are so many and wonderful that no effort is here made to describe them.] Let him sink (when no longer can he strive, though his tongue be bitten through with the effort and the blood gush from his nostrils) into the blackness of unconsciousness, and then, on coming to himself, let him write down soberly and accurately a record of all that hath occurred, yea a record of all that hath occurred.

EXPLICIT

CHAPTER 10

THE QABALAH

The Qabalah is best studied in the books like *Kaballah Unveiled* by S. L. MacGregor-Mathers, *Mystical Qabala* by Dion Fortune, and *The Tree of Life* by Israel Regardie. I could not presume to compare with these three classics in this chapter. Needless to mention, these books should be studied as textbooks, as described in chapter 4. Additionally, a copy of *777 and Other Qabalistic Writings* by Aleister Crowley is a must, as an indispensible reference. This book was created as a tool, and is used to confirm experiences during ritual as genuine, or as imagination. A list of recommended Qabalistic reading is provided at the end of this chapter, but these three books should take a good deal of time to study thoroughly.

It should be noted that the Qabalah, studied for purposes of using it as a tool in the practice of ritual magick, was not its original purpose in early history. It is the third book of the Jewish religion, the first being The Torah, and the second being The Talmud. It was only to be studied by married Rabbis over age 40, whose maturity would prevent them from having their heads turned by the mystical powers which may be generated. It has been suggested that Moses was a student of the Qabalah in the courts of the Pharoah, and he in turn brought the teachings forth, as he liberated the Jews from the land of Egypt. References to the Qabalah may be found in the most ancient of Egyptian historical records, which supports the claim of its unfounded antiquity.

The word "Qabalah" means literally "to receive." The most complete definition of the Qabalah is that given by Aleister Crowley in 777. Qabalah is:

A) A language fitted to describe certain classes of phenomena, and to express certain classes of ideas which escape regular phraseology. You might as well object to the technical terminology of chemistry.

B) An unsectarian and elastic terminology by means of which it is possible to equate the mental processes of people apparently diverse owing to the constraint imposed upon them by the peculiarities of their literary expression. You might as well object to a lexicon, or a treatise on comparative religion.

C) A system of symbolism which enables thinkers to formulate their ideas with complete precision, and to find simple expression for complex thoughts, especially such as include previously disconnected orders of conception. You might as well object to algebraic symbols.

D) An instrument for interpreting symbols whose meaning has become obscure, forgotten or misunderstood by establishing a necessary connection between the essence of forms, sounds, simple ideas (such as number) and their spiritual, moral, or intellectual equivalents. You might as well object to interpreting ancient art by consideration of beauty as determined by physiological facts.

E) A system of classification of omniform ideas so as to enable the mind to increase its vocabulary of thoughts and facts through organizing and correlating them. You might as well object to the mnemonic value of Arabic modifications of roots.

F) An instrument for proceeding from the known to the unknown on similar principles to those of mathematics. You might as well object to the use of $\sqrt{-1}$, x^4, etc.

G) A system of criteria by which the truth of correspondences may be tested with a view to criticizing new discoveries in the light of their coherence with the whole body of truth. You might as well object to judging character and status by educational and social convention.[1]

The ritual magician utilizes practical aspects of the system, based on the study of the Qabalah in the form of The Tree of Life glyph (see figure 20 on page 110). The system used may be described as a storage system for the classification of all things, from an atomic particle to the universe. Israel Regardie describes The Tree of Life as a file cabinet to contain the Universe.[2] Mainly, the ritual magician utilizes the classification of certain physical things (such as numbers, words, colors, odors, weapons, animals, etc.) to establish a link with the corresponding planetary forces or celestial influences; although the list of possible benefits of studying the Qabalah is endless, this is the main concern of the novice ritual magician.

The Tree of Life glyph is a series of ten spheres, or Sephiroth interconnected with twenty-two lines, or Paths (see figure 20). Each Sephiroth is named and numbered from 1 to 10, and is representative of certain forces and influences, among countless other symbolisms. Each Path is numbered from 11 to 32 and each also represents a myriad of symbolisms, many of which are collected in the tables of *777 and Other Qabalistic Writings* by Crowley. The Tree is said to emerge from a triad of emanations, traditionally depicted as being above Kether, and named Ain (which translates as "nothing" or "less"), Ain Soph ("limitless"), and Ain Soph Aur ("limitless light").

It would require more than the contents of this entire book to detail this system in an adequate manner. A thor-

---

[1]Alesiter Crowley, *777 and Other Qabalistic Writings* (York Beach, ME: Samuel Weiser, 1970), Appendix A, pp. 125–126.
[2]Israel Regardie, *The Garden of Pomegranates* (London: Aries Press, 1932), p. 37.

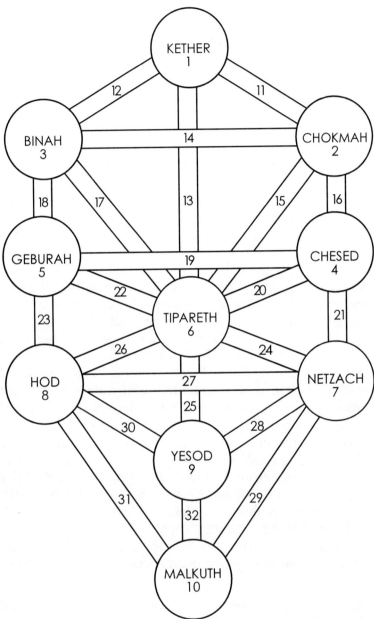

Figure 20. The Tree of Life.

ough study of the books mentioned earlier will help provide a working knowledge of the history, structure, and magickal properties of the Qabalah.

It is recommended that every student of the magickal arts "construct" a Tree of Life. This should be done on paper, in a separate Qabalistic notebook, which should be expanded regularly, referred to, and studied often. Included in this notebook should be the formula breakdown of every God-name known by the magician, examples of which may be found in *Magick in Theory and Practice*.[3] This notebook should also include a personal "Sepher Sephiroth," an example of which can be found in the third section of *777 and Other Qabalistic Writings*. Starting the procedure with traditional correspondences, the student should add every detail and thought of life to some attribute of one section of the Tree, and record them according to personal beliefs. These correspondences may change as the student progresses and determines previous impressions to be inappropriate.

Additionally, a series of four portraits of the Tree of Life are desirable for meditative and contemplative purposes. Each should be painted on canvas of adequate dimension (18" x 24", or larger), with one depicting the sephiroth and paths in the King Scale of color, one in the Queen Scale, one in the Emperor Scale and the last in the Empress Scale.[4]

The following is A Qabalistic Treatise, a series of ten poems based on and composed of the correspondences listed in the columns of *777*. Memorization of these poems may aid students in the initial construction of their own Tree. The poems may also help students memorize the majority of primary correspondences listed.

---

[3]Also see Appendix A of my book.
[4]As listed in *777 and Other Qabalistic Writings*, pp. 67–77.

A Qabalistic Treatise

Kether

Out of the infinite swirlings
    grows a crown of pre-existence
where all life begins to begin
    and continues in it's persistence
through the veils of resistance
    along the path of creation,
until "I AM THAT I AM"
    becomes the final realization.

The archangel Metatron
    armed with the Hammer of Thor
stands by Zeus and Jupiter
    of Graeco Roman folklore,
protectors of the magickal core
    (Sephiroth of conception).
For your soul to attain this goal
    you must transcend your reflection.

A pure diamond brilliance
    or an almond in flower,
symbolic correspondence
    of the ultimate power
which may create or devour,
    for one is but the other
by the God that is neither
    the Father, nor the Mother.

Profile of a bearded king
    and strong ambergris perfume,
your senses know reality
    or so you would assume;
but all I can presume
    is there's only one truth:
MALKUTH IS WITHIN KETHER,
    AS KETHER IS IN MALKUTH.

Chokmah

The supernal wisdom
    we try to aspire,
for to have knowledge of
    is to desire
everything in the zodiac
    and in all fixed stars.

Invoke Thoth and Amoun
    by unspeakable word,
TETRAGRAMMATON.
    Wisest of lords
armed with inner robes of glory,
    not scimitars.

See God face to face
    robed in pure soft blue
growing amaranth, laced
    in musk perfume
and a star ruby lying in turquoise sand.

These are the keys
    to hidden wisdom.
Ask mighty Odin,
    father Scandinavian.
He knows well
    most clever of animals,
MAN!

Binah

A queen, veiled in black and throned,
    of divine femininity.
Understanding; The silver crone
    that possesses an ability
to comprehend all great unknown
    secrets of the Holy Trinity.

Saturn's rings shine above the head
    of the matron of Qabala.
She rules the underworld and dead,
    robed in Yoni, concealed in fauna
(opium poppies of crimson red)
    and seduced by beladonna.

For Isis and the Virgin Mary
    smell sweetly in essence of myrrh.
Mothers of Gods, yet quite contrary,
    their visions of sorrow both clear.
Cybele, Juno, they all reign fairly
    and all are loved, worshiped and feared.

Chesed

Adorn yourself in deep purple and blue.
    Wear amethysts, sapphires, stones of virtue
to ask Poseidon for his secret key:
    an olive wand or crook of mercy,
accompanied by its visual match
    of a unicorn in a shamrock patch.
Now add the scent of cedar to the air,
    for success in the rest of this spell is rare.
Then strive to attain your vision of love
    before attempting to voyage above
and beyond the unmeasurable abyss

of confusion, forever bottomless!
Its gate lies in Jupiter's great red sea
    completely shrouded in mystery;
and the angels who guard this experience
    are brilliant ones demanding obedience.

Geburah

All the dark spirits of strength or might
    are symbols of form and restriction.
They balance out the forces of light
    by properly using discipline
as a tool to destroy the great myth, sin.

Thor is master of thunder's power
    and guardian of the sacred oak;
with his five-petal rose or flower
    and the odor of tobacco smoke,
he represents courage to common folk.

Except when using its nettle-like sting,
    basilisks kill without leaving scars.
One stands watch by the ruby-red ring
    I found on the scarlet sands of Mars
as I laid back to gaze at falling stars.

Fiery serpents will induce fear,
    as does Hades—king in worlds of pain.
Know that his weapons include a spear,
    a sword, a scourge, and also a chain;
but justice is the queen in his domain.

Tiphereth

When I see the Sun rise, it comes as no suprise
    that Sol should be its name,
for the spirit of man just as easily can
    be called the very same.

Apollo rides on high to wake the sleeping sky
    with beauty that light brings.
Knowing the star above inspires your vision of
    the harmony of things.

A crucified God gives our majestic king his
    rosy cross to lay on;
to learn the formula of Abrahadabra,
    word of the new Aeon.

The phoenix starts singing to Mikhael, who's bringing
    alcohol-laced coffee
to where we stopped to rest in Acacia forest
    by a bay laurel tree.

A child rides a lion, while the yellow diamond
    sets in rose pink and gold.
Pyramids of topaz sparkle on the beach as
    Ra's mysteries unfold.

Crucifixion is not too often fully taught
    as the grand sacrifice
that allows you to grow, so at last you can know
    the great work of your life.

Netzach

Self-sacrifice is what leads to victory,
    or so I've heard it said;
for it was the blood of Aphrodite
    that changed the white rose to red.
Even now, her memory hasn't faded;
    but not one of sorrow. Her death created
a vision of beauty triumphant, instead.

Embracing in an emerald circle,
    bathed in Venus' light,
Hathoor with a lamp, and Freya engirdled
    indulge in animal delights.
Such beautiful Gods, yet neither one frail.
    They are both masculine types of female,
and more than willing to make love or to fight.

A beautiful naked woman strokes a lynx
    that purrs with devotion,
as her natural creative instincts
    (flowing in perpetual motion)
silently burns, like the king's amber candle
    anointed with benzoin and red sandal,
in a great eternal flame of emotion.

Hod

Learn to display your orange and violet features
    so as to attract the silent inner teachers
who help you to recognize the sensation
    of your internal vibrations,
or nature's reverberation;
    and they reveal the realization
that the vision of splendor we strive for
    is what lifts us above every mundane creature.

No one will ever know how many souls have tried
    to pass Anubis and the jackals by his side,
just to meet their doom on the blood-stained
    and dark path of truthfulness and pain;
but the versicles, apron and names
    are unknown keys, with which we can gain
intellectual powers needed to survive,
    so you can interpret the images Thoth provides.

On Mercury, as I bask in the Sun's presence,
    an hermaphrodite inhales storax incense,
and stares into an opal on fire,
    hoping to glimpse his secret desire;
while Loki lights a viking's pyre,
    where flames of glory soar higher
than our "emotional" thoughts and "rational" sense
    that delays our union with the divine essence.

Yesod

As you run in the night
    searching for your lost dreams,
watch the hiding star's light
    descend in moon-beams.
Down to a quartz foundation,
    where you stop to wait
for the elephants
    and exotic scents
that are keys to the astral gate.

Sandals and violet veils
    enhance the Goddess Diana
in a garden of banyan,
    mandrake and damiana.
She wears perfumes of jasmine
    and ginseng root,
as Zeus, who's aglow
    in deep indigo,
serenades her with his flute.

Be aware that your ego
    is just a false face
your true self shows the world
    in its place.
All facts are mere deceptions,
    and illusions grand;
so drink orchid tea,
    it helps you to see
the image of a strong naked man.

Malkuth

Immortal spirits freely roam
    across the terraplane
in golems of flesh and bone.
    It's all just a silly game.

Time goes by, and the body dies;
    but its soul of fire,
like Osiris, again does rise.
    When will your time expire?

Other worlds exist above
    and below our dominion,
where the only law is Love.
    Anyway, that's my opinion.

While burning dittany of crete,
    flaming visions may tell
of spells to use, so you can meet
    your Holy Guardian Angel.

Wild lilies grow around
    a shady willow tree.
There a young woman, veiled and crowned,
    forms the image that you see.

Clouds of swirling yellow sand
    conceals the sleeping sphinx,
while in control of Earth is man.
    At least, that's what he thinks.

Awaiting his rebirth from
    an ivy-covered prison,
to re-appear within the kingdom.
    The Serpent has arisen!

From the Tree of Life, he dangles;
    teaching why and how to use
magic circles and triangles.
    He's got nothing left to lose.

Like puppets on a string,
    all of the people play
at being fools and kings.
    Either way, it's all the same.

You spin the wheel of life,
    hoping to win fortune and fame.
But, if you don't, that's alright.
    After all, it's just a game.

Recommended Reading

Anatomy of the Body of God (Frater Achad)
The Garden of Pomegranates (Israel Regardie)
Godwin's Cabalistic Encyclopedia (David Godwin)
The Holy Kabbalah (A. E. Waite)
An Introduction to Kaballah (W. Wynn Westcott)
Kabbala of Numbers (Sephariel)
Magic and the Qabalah (W. E. Butler)
The Middle Pillar (Israel Regardie)
The Practical Guide to Qabalistic Symbolism (Gareth Knight)
Secret Wisdom of the Qabala (J. F. C. Fuller)
Sepher Yetzirah (various translations)
The Tree of Life (Israel Regardie)
The Zohar (various translations)

CHAPTER 11

WEAPONS OF THE ART

When performing an act of magick, the ritual magician utilizes certain tools (weapons, instruments) in order to employ the forces of nature to effect some kind of change (see figures 21–24 on pages 124–127). The forces referred to can be categorized into four elemental groups, and classified as the forces of earth, air, water and fire. These groups are all composed of different forms of energy, and each possess separate attributes and characteristics. In addition, each force is sympathetic to a certain "weapon." That is to say, the forces may be influenced or directed by the proper usage of what are known as the elemental weapons. There are four weapons which should be considered the minimum armory of the magician.

The disk is utilized to employ the forces of earth. The original use of the disk was as a shield. Its purpose was strictly defensive, mainly to absorb or deflect opposing force. Traditionally, disks were made out of some kind of metal, such as gold or silver, with a pentagram or hexagram etched on its surface. It is also permissible to make one out of wood.[1] It is recommended that the disk be from five to ten inches in diameter.

Magickally, it is used to slow or block another force by the application of the earth forces, which are very dense and unyielding. In actuality, the tool is as inert as the element earth, itself. Other than to invoke earth, it would be a very rare occasion that you would deem it necessary to use

---

[1] Israel Regardie suggests wood in *The Golden Dawn*.

FIRE WAND

AIR DAGGER

WATER CUP

EARTH DISK

Figure 21. The Magickal Weapons of the Order of the Golden Dawn.

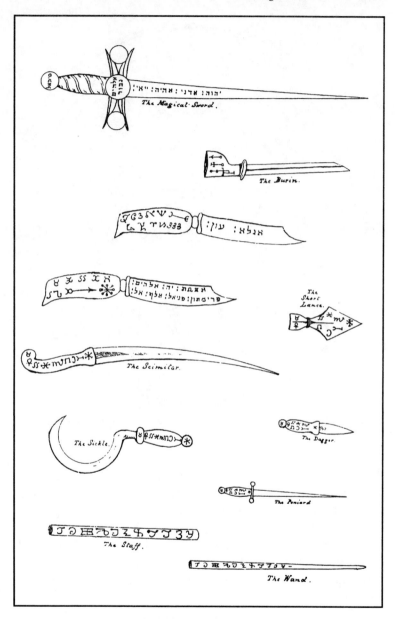

Figure 22. The Magickal Weapons from *The Key of Solomon the King*.

Figure 23. The Disk of Frater Achad, from *Gems from the Equinox*, p. 729.

the pantacle (another name for the disk) in order to advance your progress, being that the nature of the earth energy is to slow, or even stop other forces. And magicians almost always seek to bring on change more quickly, rather than slowing it down. In actual usage, the disk is mainly needed to provide balance and equilibrium on the altar, as the physical representation of the forces of earth within the circle.

The disk does not actually conduct energy, although it is capable of absorbing a great amount of energy and storing it, if the energy is properly "trapped" within

Figure 24. The Disk of the Serpent.

it.[2] Disks are considered passive or "negative" because of their natural tendency to affect active or "positive" energy by attracting and absorbing it, in order to balance out their own "negativity." In addition, the round shape of the disk is symbolic of the feminine aspects it possesses. That is, in representation of Mother Earth as the great womb that can absorb all of the other forces.

The dagger is used to employ the forces of air. A smaller version of the sword, both were originally almost

---

[2]This is the basis for effective methods of charging talismans, which will be discussed in chapter 15.

identical in usage. A sword is required for evocationary work. Economically, the dagger is more practical and usually satisfactory, but it is advantageous to have a sword in certain cases. Magickally, the dagger is used to banish any and all influences, either negative or positive, and is mainly used prior to and after a magickal ritual performance.

The forces of air are considered to be active or "positive," but basically its energy is used to disperse passive or "negative" energy. Actually, a better description would be that it attracts and absorbs the "negative" energy, mixing together to cause neutralization of both forces—self-destruction in a sense. The positivity of its force is applied to negativity in order to produce equilibrium.[3]

The cup is used to employ the forces of water. It is the symbolic representation of the Holy Grail, which contains "the blood of the Saints." The cup also represents the feminine nature of attracting and accepting masculine or "positive" forces. It is said that feminine energy flows inward, toward the center, and its flow draws other energy inward along with it. The other forces are attracted to the natural flowing energy. The forces of water are said to be passive, because it accepts all of the positive energy that it can attract.

Magickally, the cup is well-suited for works such as invocations, where you attract a certain force into your circle.[4] Although its presence may be required, it is almost never suitable for works such as evocations.

The wand is used to utilize the forces of fire. It is probably the most well-known weapon associated with magick. In fact, going back in history, we may note that the first weapon used by human beings, in an offensive manner, was the club.

People know well of non-magickal uses of daggers, swords, and shields. Also, the sacred chalices go back at

---

[3]As if a math equation $(+) + (-) = 0$.

[4]The cup is a circle, when seen from above.

least into ancient Egyptian history. So we know that these are all ancient weapons of art and war. Swords and cups were always ornamented, and shields were emblazoned with symbols of the tribes, family, or Gods of the warrior.

The wand, on the other hand, has always been the most basic of weapons and represents the original source of fire. Magickally, as a tool, it is used to direct the most basic and powerful of the elemental forces. These forces can be dangerously overpowering and could conceivably cause the complete destruction of any person who is not in complete control of the situation.

So basic, in fact, is the wand, that in use it should be considered an extension of your hand, as it directs the purest of human powers. These powers are generally overly active and so positive that once in motion, if not checked, will drain every bit of lifeforce from a human body. In a sense, the wand could be considered the barrel through which we aim and fire our magickal energy. It is the hollow tube or pipe that, when inserted into the earth, strikes the hidden pool of energy underground, releasing the pressure and allowing the flow to gush upward in a geyser of power.

Now that we have discussed these four elemental weapons, it becomes necessary to make mention of another magickal weapon. This is the most important tool of magick, because with it you shall create all of the other weapons; and additionally, it stores all of your own personal magickal energy, ready to be used at any moment. It has been known as "The Temple of The Holy Ghost," "Tomb of Osiris," and "The Chariot of our Lady Babalon," and is in fact, our own physical body.

To illustrate how all these things are tied together; consider the wand placed in the south, the cup in the west, the dagger in the east and the disk in the north. They are physical representations of the four worlds that surround you. Your body stands in the center, a combination of all the forces. It is the center of the universe and/or the tip of the pyramid, with each side representing one of the elements that all converge to produce your body in its solidity and materiality. You are both the source of your own personal magickal energy as well as a receptacle for any force that you can make yourself fit to attract and absorb. Your link with any of the elemental worlds is its corresponding weapon. These allow you to influence these worlds, and also allow them to influence you. They could be considered the keys to the gates of the elemental worlds, although they are only a part of the key. Other factors are involved.

These weapons should not only symbolize their respective elemental worlds, but they are also representations of or extensions of yourself. They should reflect your nature; for instance, a flamboyant individual should create or possess heavily ornamented weapons. A quiet and reserved person's weapons should be more on the plain side, and less ornamented.

Practicality dictates that you purchase the cup and dagger (unless you are a skilled metalworker), and probably at least the materials for the disk and wand. Remember not to argue about the price, or try to talk the merchant down. This reduces the value of your weapons. They should be weapons that you can be proud to have, not proud of yourself for buying cheaply. There are other traditional reasons not to haggle over the price, which we need not go into here.

Your weapons should be personalized by you in some way. In *Liber A vel Armorum*, Aleister Crowley suggests that you first devise, and then:

- Engrave a symbol to represent the universe on your disk;

- Engrave a word to represent the universe on your dagger;

- Engrave a number to represent the universe on your cup;

- Perform a deed to represent the universe in such a way as to include the wand.[5]

Additionally, when each magickal tool is first acquired or constructed, the magician should immediately sprinkle each with hyssop-treated water while speaking words of purification, and then rub it with Abramelin Oil while speaking the words of consecration.[6] The magician should then promptly wrap each in a black silk cloth, conceal them in a secluded place, and leave them untouched for thirty days.

As a general rule, the magician should always acquire and consecrate magickal weapons on a Wednesday. The exception to that rule is the black-handled dagger, which is used for banishing rituals. This should be acquired and consecrated on a Saturday.

Any accouterment utilized during ritual should be considered a magickal tool, and treated as such. This includes the robe, the altar, censer, candles, candlesticks and the assorted dishes and vials. All tools should be regularly purified and consecrated as described earlier, especially prior to any magickal operation. Each item should be kept individually wrapped in silk cloth, in a color corresponding to its elemental symbolism.[7] All items should be kept concealed in a secluded place, never to be displayed or handled by anyone, except by the magician, during ritual.

---

[5] "Liber A vel Armorum" in *Magick in Theory and Practice* (New York: Castle Books, n.d.), p. 435.

[6] The words of purification and consecration are mentioned in chapter 2.

[7] The wand in red, the cup in blue, the dagger in yellow, and the disk in black. White silk is suitable for all other implements, including the robe and altar.

If you claim the title of magician, aspiring or otherwise, you should complete your armory of weapons during the first year of practice. Lack of these tools does not deter the magician from study and rehearsal of any theory or rituals. In fact, any of these tools may be easily constructed for rehearsal purposes.[8] As soon as possible, however, you should construct your own personalized and permanent magickal weapons for performing works of the Art.

---

[8]For example, a disk may be a pentagram drawn on a piece of paper, a dagger may be a kitchen knife, a cup from out of the cupboard and a new unsharpened pencil will suffice as a wand.

CHAPTER 12

A LUNAR INVOCATION

The following is an invocation of the forces of Luna, which, when properly performed, greatly improves astral abilities and illuminates you with the forces of illusion. This invoca-

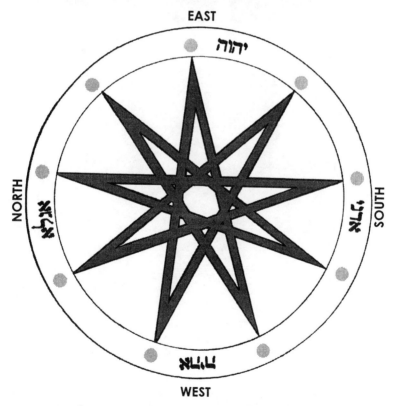

Figure 25. The Circle of Lunar Invocation. The star would be colored indigo blue. The colored dots around the star represent violet candles.

Figure 26. Altar Setup for Lunar Invocation. In the East (bottom of figure) is the candle, censer, dagger; in the West (top) is water, candle, cup; in the North (right) is the disk, candle, salt; in the South is oil, candle, wand. The Tree of Life has been painted on the front of this altar.

tion should be performed on a monthly basis, at the moment of the full moon.[1]

1) Prepare the temple:

A. On the floor of the temple, prepare a white circle with two black border lines, and the God-names of the four quarters in black within the borders. These shall be in their respective directions [YHVH in the east, ADNI in the south, AHIH in the west, and AGLA in the north], and in Hebrew letters [See figure 25 on page 133]. The circle should be at least six feet in diameter, but nine feet wide would be better. [Ideally, one should use charcoal on a white concrete floor. However, an acceptable substitution would be on a large piece of plywood. One should first paint the whole piece white, before painting the God-names in black.]

B. Paint a nine-pointed star in the circle. This should be painted indigo blue, and the tips of the star should just touch the inner border of the circle.

C. Place one violet candle at the tip of each point of the star, and within the inner and outer borders of the circle.

D. Arrange the altar in the center of the circle, with the front of it facing the east. See figure 26 on page 134. [The robe, altar and every object involved in this ritual should be purified and consecrated no more than twelve hours prior to the ritual bathing, as described in chapter 2. This may be done while preparing the temple.]

E. Arrange four white candles on top of the altar, in each of the four directions [north, south, east and west].

F. Next to each candle on the altar should be the appropriate magickal weapon [disk in north, wand in south, dagger in east and cup in west].

---

[1]Complete this text before performing any invocations outlined herein. There is a great deal of vital information regarding ritual performance in future chapters.

G. Place a vial of oil [Abramelin Oil is best, but pure virgin olive oil will do] next to the candle in the south, a vial of natural water [ocean or spring water] next to the candle in the west, a dish of natural salt [sea or rock salt] next to the candle in the north and the censer next to the candle in the east.

H. Use jasmine or ginseng incense.

2) Prepare yourself:

A. You should have been performing each of the rituals outlined in chapter 4 daily, and also meditating daily, for several months previous to the performance of this ritual.

B. Study pictures or statues of all Lunar goddesses, such as Luna, Diana and Shu, until their images are firmly fixed in your mind. Also, read any information regarding them you can find. Frazer's *Golden Bough* is an excellent reference and I'm sure the local library has many volumes regarding mythical figures.

C. The best time to perform this particular invocation is on a full moon. Try to plan on as close to the exact time of the full moon [check the weather bureau or newspaper] before the change. If you can, try to time this so you complete the ritual at the moment of the full moon.

D. After preparing the temple, wait until approximately thirty minutes before the designated time for the beginning of the ritual, and then take a nice long bath using water that has been treated with hyssop and a few drops of jasmine oil. Relax and clear your mind. Allow all thoughts to flow away with the water. Several times during the bathing, speak the words of consecration. ["Asperges me, AHIEH (vibrate), Hyssoppo et mundabor. Lavabis me et super nivem dealbabor."]

E. After the bathing, consecrate yourself with Abramelin Oil. Use your right forefinger to make the sign of the Rose Cross over your heart, while speaking the words of consecration. ["Accendat in nobis ADNI (vibrate) ignem sui amoris et flammam aeternae caritatis."]

F. Now clear your mind in meditation for a few minutes, then put on your robe [a black robe of either cotton or silk is always suitable for the uninitiated] and the lunar amulet, which will be described in chapter 15. You are now ready to move to the circle area, and begin the invocation.

3) Perform the Banishing Ritual of the Serpent.

4) After the banishing, move to the west side of the altar facing the east. Then move deosil (clockwise) around the altar, to the south. Light the white candle there and moving deosil, light the other three. Then return to the west side of altar, facing east, always moving deosil.

5) Move deosil to the east side of the altar and light the incense in the censer. Then move to the easternmost violet candle and light it. Moving deosil, light the other eight candles around the circle, and then move back to the west side of the altar, facing east.

6) With the butt of the dagger, strike the altar once and state "I am (your name and grades, if any)."

7) State the oath: "Hear me and know that I am now going to invoke the spirit and power of LUNA, so I may obtain the Vision of the Machinery of the Universe, learn of the forces of illusion, and to improve my abilities on the astral plane. I will not leave this circle until I succeed in this operation because it is necessary for me to progress in my spiritual attainment!" Then, knock once with the butt of the dagger on the altar.

8) Now walk around the altar to your left and move to the easternmost point of the circle. Make a sharp right turn

and circumbulate [walk around the circle, just inside the border] deosil for nine revolutions, making the sign of "Horus or the enterer" in the east. [With your hands drawn back to the sides of your head, move your left foot forward approximately twelve inches, and allow your hands to shoot forward in front of you, let them spread out and then allow them to return to your sides. See also figure 10 on page 35. Additionally, when performing this sign, one should also assume the God-form of Horus, as described in Appendix B.] Stop after the ninth circumbulation and return (always moving deosil) to the west side of the altar, facing east.

9) Pick up the wand in your right hand and the cup in your left. Hold them over head and knock them together nine times in three batteries of three (knock 3 times, pause, knock 3 times, pause, and knock 3 times). Then begin the conjurations. (At this point, assume the God-form of Shu, as described in Appendix B, and maintain that form through Step 10.)

> The circle is cast,
> 　　all visions beyond have vanished.
> Every spirit and specter
> 　　has been properly banished.
> Gone are all my earthly thoughts
> 　　and delusions,
> as I wait to experience
> 　　the forces of illusion.
> LUNA, I invoke thee!
> 　　Descend and illuminate me.
>
> From the roots of Yesod,
> 　　my spirit will flower
> as I glimpse the reflections
> 　　of divine power.
> Descend now Luna,

in accordance with my will.
I am an empty void
    that only you can fill.
LUNA, I invoke thee!
    Descend and illuminate me.

Hear me as I call:
    Luna! Diana! Shu!
Come lift me up
    out of the terrestial stew.
Come forth to aid and guard me
    in this work of the art,
and fulfill the desires
    that burn in my heart.
LUNA, I invoke thee!
    Descend and illuminate me.

Descend now Luna,
    I welcome your embrace.
Show me what lies behind this mask,
    my false face.
Alone in space,
    I await the presence of your might.
Descend now Luna,
    fill my circle with your light.
LUNA, I invoke thee!
    Descend and illuminate me.

10) Then, with your wand, make the Invoking Hexagram of Luna overhead while vibrating ARARITA. Then touch wand to the center of the hexagram and vibrate SHADAI EL CHAI. And then, the forces of Luna shall fill your circle and completely envelope everything in the confines with lunar energy. Bask in the power and absorb all the energy that flows toward you.

11) Closing the temple:

A. When the time is right, rise (if you are sitting) and extinguish the violet candles, starting in the east and moving widdershins (counterclockwise); and then, still moving widdershins, return to the west side of the altar and face east.

B. Perform the Banishing Ritual of the Serpent.

C. Hold your dagger above your head and say, "And now I say unto thee, depart in peace unto thine habitations and abodes—and may the blessings of the highest be upon thee in the name of (vibrate) ARARITA—SHADAI EL CHAI, and let there be peace between thee and me; and be thou very ready to come, whensoever thou art invoked and called, either by a word, or by a will or by this mighty conjuration of Magick Art."

D. Then with the butt of the dagger, strike the top of the altar ten times. First 3 times, pause, then 4 times, pause, then 3 times, and say, "I now declare this temple duly closed." Then strike the altar once.

As described in chapter 2, after the final closing, you should then leave the circle area for at least one hour, presumably to document the event in your magickal records. You should then return, and perform the Lesser Banishing Ritual of the Pentagram, and the Lesser Banishing Ritual of the Hexagram. Then you should remove all evidence of the ritual.

CHAPTER 13

PRELIMINARIES AND CLOSINGS

The system of magick outlined throughout this book is a variation of the qabalistic system; more so, it is a mere branch of the qabalistic tree. By making a serious study of the books mentioned in chapter 10 you should soon develop a working knowledge of this system, or at least a partial grasp of the basic concepts. Rituals based on this system must follow a certain outline, which the magician works with, actually constructing the ritual around (or building on) that outline, illustrated in Table 3 on page 142.

The four periods of a ritual, as discussed in chapter 2, are a part of that outline on a grand scale. The creation period is purely spontaneous in every case,[1] and no rigid laws may be applied to it. The preparation is determined by the standards of the system to which the operation belongs, be they Solomonic, Enochian, Abramelin's, Golden Dawn, or what have you.[2] The performance itself, likewise must be devised according to its governing system.

Any Qabalistic ritual must begin with first, the purification, second, the consecration, and third, a banishing. Correspondingly, the ritual must end with a banishing, the release, and the closing. The matter between these six steps may be any number of steps, even just one. However, these preliminaries and closing steps are essential factors to the success of any Qabalistic ritual. Their importance cannot be overly emphasized. Every logical

---

[1]Or should be. There has been the occasional case of a fellow magician attempting to "plant" or encourage some ritual, possibly for malignant purposes.
[2]Many systems are offshoots of the Qabalistic, and these are governed by its laws.

Table 3. Outline of the Qabalistic Ritual Structure.

I. THE CREATION

II. THE PREPARATION

1. Find the location.

2. Gather the materials.

3. Memorize the instructions.

4. Choose an appropriate date and time.

III. THE PERFORMANCE

1. Purification.

2. Consecration.

3. Banishing.

4. The ritual, to be performed in the following order:
   - Light the candles and incense.
   - Make the oath.
   - Perform the circumambulations.
   - Sound the knocks or knells.
   - Recite the incantations.
   - Draw the symbols.
   - Vibrate the God-names.
   - Assume the God-form.
   - Experience any initial reaction.

5. Banishing.

6. Release.

7. Closing.

IV. THE RESULTS

1. The next day.

2. A week later.

3. A month later.

act must first begin, and lastly end. The ritual could not be considered complete before the final steps required to end it are accomplished. Without a proper ending, the whole ritual would have to be considered a waste of time and effort.

The magickal ritual should exist as does a "life," which begins at birth and ends in death. Although, under close examination, a life truly begins with "creation," and then "preparation" before the birth; and after the death, the impressions of its existence should continue to be experienced. When a ritual is created, the performance should breathe life into that ritual, and its results should continue to manifest long after the act has been completed.

Chapter 14

A MERCURIAL INVOCATION

The invocation of Mercury, when properly performed, greatly improves your ability to comprehend difficult subject matter, and interpret veiled mysteries from complicated texts. This invocation should be performed whenever Mercury's orbit brings it close to Earth. (In fact, the ritual magician should keep track of the paths of all celestial bodies, and perform appropriate invocations at every opportunity.)

1. Prepare the temple:

A. Prepare the circle as in Step 1-A of "A Lunar Invocation," in chapter 12.

B. Paint an eight-pointed star in the circle. This should be painted violet purple, and the tips of the star should just touch the inner border of the circle.

C. One orange candle should be placed at the tip of each point of the star, and within the inner and outer borders of the circle.

D. Arrange the altar in the center of the circle, with the front of it facing east.

E. Arrange four white candles on top of the altar, in each of the four directions.

F. Next to each candle on the altar should be the appropriate magickal weapon.

G. Place a vial of oil next to the candle in the south, a vial of natural water next to the candle in the west, a dish of natural salt next to the candle in the north and the censer next to the candle in the east.

H. Storax (stacte) incense should be used, however good abramelin incense should be partly composed of storax, and would also be suitable, besides providing a much nicer odor. (Abramelin incense is composed of lignum aloes, storax and olibanum.)

2. Prepare yourself:

A. You should have been performing each of the rituals outlined in chapter 4 daily, and also meditating daily, for several months previous to the performance of this ritual.

B. Study pictures or statues of all the Mercurial gods, such as Mercury, Hermes, and Thoth, until their images are firmly fixed in your mind. Also, read any information regarding them you can find in books on mythological figures.

C. The best time to perform this particular invocation is at a time when Mercury is visible in the evening sky. A good astrologer, or a well-equipped weather bureau, can predict the moment when Mercury will draw near Earth.

D. After preparing the temple, wait until approximately thirty minutes before the designated time for the beginning of the ritual, and then take a nice long bath using water that has been treated with hyssop and a few drops of Abramelin Oil. Relax and clear your mind. Allow all thoughts to flow away with the water. Several times during the bathing, speak the words of consecration.

E. After the bathing, consecrate yourself with Abramelin Oil. Use your right forefinger to make the sign of the Rose Cross over your heart, while speaking the words of consecration.

F. Now clear your mind in meditation for a few minutes, and then put on your robe, and the mercurial amulet, which will be described in chapter 15. You are now ready to move to the circle area, and begin the invocation.

3. Perform the Banishing Ritual of the Serpent.

4. After the banishing, move to the west side of the altar facing the east. Then move deosil around the altar, to the south. Light the white candle there and moving deosil, light the other three. Then return to the west side of altar, facing east, always moving deosil.

5. Move deosil to the east side of the altar and light the incense in the censer. Then move to the easternmost orange candle and light it. Moving deosil, light the other seven candles around the circle, and then move back to the west side of the altar, facing east.

6. With the butt of the dagger, strike the altar once and state "I am (your name and grades, if any)."

7. State the oath: "Hear me and know that I am now going to invoke the spirit and power of MERCURY, so I may obtain the Vision of Splendor, learn of the forces of the mind, and improve my abilities to comprehend the learned teachings. I will not leave this circle until I succeed in this operation because it is necessary for me to progress in my spiritual attainment!" Then, knock once with the butt of the dagger on the altar.

8. Now walk around the altar to your left and move to the easternmost point of the circle. Make a sharp right turn and circumambulate deosil for eight revolutions, making the sign of Horus or The Enterer in the east. Stop after the eighth circumambulation and return (always moving deosil) to the west side of the altar, facing east.

9. Pick up the wand in your right hand and the cup in your left. Hold them over head and knock them together eight times in two batteries of three, divided by one of two (knock 3 times, pause, knock 2 times, pause, and knock 3

times). Then begin the conjurations. (At this point, the magician should assume the God-form of Thoth, as described in Appendix B, and maintain that form through Step 10.)

> From the center of this Circle of the Art,
>> with willing spirit and a pounding heart,
> I stand prepared to part the veil
>> between the heavens and the earth,
> and take firm hold of the Serpent's tail
>> which devours my soul, then inspires my rebirth.
> MERCURY, I invoke Thee!
>> Descend and educate me.
>
> As the words are uttered, and the symbols drawn
>> to be heard and seen in the realm beyond
> by those whose names, I now do speak.
>> Ye Gods of ancient histories
> who keep secret that which I now seek:
>> the key that unlocks forbidden mysteries.
> MERCURY, I invoke Thee!
>> Descend and educate me.
>
> Seething, ghostly vapours rise in orange tinted smoke,
>> as the secret signs and gestures invoke
> the purest of hermetic force,
>> to the vessel which I've made fit.
> Attracting such from its mystic source
>> downward, here to this barren, earthly pit.
> MERCURY, I invoke Thee!
>> Descend and educate me.
>
> The skies divide, and streaming violet rays descend.
>> I glimpse the Vision of Splendour, and then
> seering heat and a blinding light
>> from the depths of the flaming sun,
> shall consume this body with its might

in a most glorious annihilation.
MERCURY, I invoke Thee!
Descend and educate me.

10. Then, with your wand, make the Invoking Hexagram of Mercury overhead while vibrating "ARARITA." Then touch wand to the center of the hexagram and vibrate "ELOHIM TZBAOTH." And then, the forces of Mercury shall fill your circle and completely envelop everything in the confines with mercurial energy. Bask in the power and absorb all the energy that flows toward you.

11. Closing the temple:

A. When the time is right, rise (if you are sitting) and extinquish the orange candles, starting in the east and moving widdershins; and then, still moving widdershins, return to the west side of the altar and face east.

B. Perform the Banishing Ritual of the Serpent.

C. Hold your dagger above your head and say, "And now I say unto thee, depart in peace unto thine habitations and abodes—and may the blessings of the highest be upon thee in the name of (vibrate) ARARITA—ELOHIM TZBAOTH, and let there be peace between thee and me; and be thou very ready to come, whensoever thou art invoked and called, either by a word, or by a will or by this mighty conjuration of Magick Art."

D. Then with the butt of the dagger, strike the top of the altar 10 times. First 3 times, pause, then 4 times, pause, then 3 times, and say, "I now declare this temple duly closed." Then strike the altar once.

Chapter 15

AMULETS AND TALISMANS

No book of the magickal art should be considered complete before thoroughly discussing the proper use of amulets and talismans. For the novice's sake, it is best to begin with an explanation of exactly what these objects are. Most people have heard of them, although few are aware of exactly what they are used for. Webster's Ninth New Collegiate Dictionary defines an amulet as "a charm (as an ornament) often inscribed with a magic incantation or symbol to protect the wearer against evil (as disease or witchcraft) or to aid him." Webster's also defines a talisman as "1: an object held to act as a charm to avert evil and bring good fortune. 2: something producing apparently magical or miraculous effects." These definitions may be adequate explanation for the mundane, however the ritual magician need be aware of the significance of both. The distinction between the two should be based upon the following criteria:

 1) An amulet is a piece of jewelry centered around a single natural stone, which possesses a particular virtue.

• An amulet may be in the form of a pendant, ring, earring, or any piece of jewelry.

• Amulets have natural virtues, and need not be charged. They do require frequent purification and consecration, as do all magickal implements, which both amulets and talismans are. However, in certain cases, when the amulet has a specific purpose, it must be charged.

2) A talisman is an object constructed by the magician from natural materials, for a specific purpose.

• Talismans are traditionally crafted from a piece of metal by engraving them with a particular sigil; although wood, leather, or parchment are also used in certain cases. A talisman may also be made of natural stone, if engraved neatly. Additionally, a talisman may be any object of natural matter, and is often something which one might not expect, such as a painting or a book.

• A talisman must be "charged" with a certain force, of either an elemental or planetary (celestial) nature.

An amulet is most frequently recognized as being in the form of a pendant. In this study the student will be required to obtain at least two in pendant form, and two in ring form. Before describing the specific requirements of these four amulets, we should briefly discuss the "virtues" of stones.

Every natural stone possesses certain virtues, which may be better described as a capacity to influence certain forces. This may be a sympathetic (ability to attract certain forces) or antipathetic (ability to repel certain forces) influence, depending on the nature of the stone itself. Although unprovable by any human standards, this theory is generally accepted as "fact" by the ritual magician, based on the writings of many notable occult authors. In the first section of his classic text, *The Magus or Celestial Intelligencer*, Francis Barrett states that, "It is common knowledge of Magicians, that stones inherit great virtues, which they recieve through the spheres and activity of the celestial influences, by the medium of the soul or spirit of the world."[1] After a brief digression regarding the opinions of other writers, he continues brilliantly by stating, "I say, that these occult virtues

---

[1]Francis Barrett, *The Magus or Celestial Intelligencer* (London: Lackington, Allen & Co., 1801) p. 39.

are disposed throughout the animal, vegetable and mineral kingdoms, by seeds, or ideas originally emanating from the Divine mind, and through supercelestial spirits and intelligence always operating, according to their proper offices and governments allotted them; which virtues are infused, as I before said, through the medium of the universal spirit, as by a general and manifest sympathy and antipathy established in the law of Nature."[2] This matter has been debated upon endlessly over the centuries, and students are bound to come across many chapters devoted to this subject in the course of their studies. Therefore, this theory should be accepted for the moment, so we may continue with the practical aspects of the discussion. This should be done with the understanding that the practice of carrying amulets will prove to be of great benefit to ritual magicians. Students are encouraged to collect many amulets of varying stones, but these four should be considered the minimum "armory" of amulets any magician should possess.

The first pendant should be a solitary quartz crystal, mounted in silver and hung from a silver chain. The size is not of great importance, although it should not be too large. This will become your lunar amulet, and upon acquiring it, you should immediately purify and consecrate it,[3] and wrap it in black silk cloth, concealing it for a period of no less than thirty days. This should all be accomplished well in advance of the first performance of the "Lunar Invocation" outlined in chapter 12, as you will need to wear this amulet for the first time during that ritual, and it should not be unwrapped until that time.[4]

The second amulet required will be a solitary fire opal, mounted in a silver ring setting, which fits the forefinger of

[2]Francis Barrett, *The Magus or Celestial Intelligencer* (London: Lackington, Allen & Co., 1801) p. 39.
[3]As you have done with the magickal weapons. Additionally, the magician should acquire and consecrate the lunar amulet on a Monday.
[4]During that invocation, no jewelry other than the lunar amulet should be worn.

your left hand. Again, the size is not of great importance, although you should pick one that displays a good "fire" quality, or flashes red when light strikes it. This will become your mercurial amulet, and should be treated as was the lunar amulet,[5] not to be unwrapped until the first performance of the "Mercurial Invocation" outlined in chapter 14, and then to be placed on your left forefinger after donning the robe.[6]

The third amulet required will be a solitary emerald, mounted in a silver ring setting, which fits the forefinger of your right hand. This will become your venutian amulet, and should be treated as the others,[7] not to be unwrapped until the first performance of the "Venutian Invocation," and then to be placed on your right forefinger after donning the robe.[8]

The fourth amulet required will be a solitary yellow topaz, mounted in gold and hung from a gold chain. This should be treated as the rest,[9] not to be unwrapped until the first performance of the "Solar Invocation." During this invocation, one is permitted to wear either just the solar amulet, or all four, if preferred.[10]

By wearing and including these amulets in your invocations, you expose them to the planetary "energies" which are invoked into the circle. The stones are subtly influenced by these forces, retaining some of the energy. Since all stones possess certain virtues inherently, as discussed earlier, this energy adds to their supply, thus increasing their overall level of energy, much like the human aura does during ritual. The stone's strength grows in accordance with

[5]The mercurial amulet should be acquired and consecrated on a Wednesday.
[6]Again, no other jewelery should be worn during that invocation.
[7]The venutian amulet should be acquired and consecrated on a Friday.
[8]Again, no other jewelry to be worn.
[9]The solar amulet should be acquired and consecrated on a Sunday.
[10]The solar amulet should rest above the lunar amulet upon your chest, so be sure both the chain's lengths allow this.

the amount of energy it is exposed to, and the regularity of its exposure. In other words, the amulet will grow stronger every time it is worn by the magician during ritual, and, correspondingly, will weaken when neglected.

As with all magickal implements, the amulets should be regularly purified and consecrated, and kept wrapped in white silk in a secluded place. They should only be worn when their effects are desired, and should never be displayed or handled by anyone, other than the magician. By wearing these amulets in the course of their daily activities, the magician attracts energies that are sympathetic to the specific stone. This attraction is at first subtle, but increases as the stone's energy grows, until one may experience similar effects to that of an invocation by simply donning the amulet. Of course, this extreme is not to be expected until after many years of regular exposure.

Either of the pendant amulets may be worn solitarily, or both at the same time; but one should never wear just one of the rings, with the solitary exception of the initial invocation, which is the first time the amulet should be worn. These should always be worn simultaneously, and may be worn in conjunction with either, both or neither of the pendants. If while being worn in public, an amulet is noticed by somebody who comments on it, the magician should skillfully change the subject, drawing all attention away from the stone. Never allow it to be focused on by another individual, as people can influence your amulet in undesirable ways, especially in the case of another magician.[11]

As described earlier, a talisman is an object which must be constructed by the magician. Although the material used is of a natural matter—metal, wood, leather, parchment—these things are all processed in some way. Metals must be

---

[11]Even the non-magician will unconsciously draw energy from an amulet, thereby weakening it and influencing it negatively with their own impurities.

I	E	M	I	M	E	I
E	R	I	O	N	T	E
M	I	R	T	I	N	M
I	O	T	I	T	O	I
M	N	I	T	R	I	M
E	T	N	O	I	R	E
I	E	M	I	M	E	I

TO TRANSFORM MEN INTO ASSES.

D	I	S	K	E	N	A	H
I							
S							
E							
K		Ω					
E							
N							
A							
H							

TO TAKE ON THE APPEARANCE
OF AN OLD WOMAN.

EXCITING EARTHQUAKES.

THE OPERATION OF INVISIBILITY.

Figure 27. Top: Examples of Talismans from *The Book of Abra-Melin, the Mage*; Bottom: Examples of Talismans from *The Key of Solomon the King*.

mined, separated and formed into the disks used for talismans. Leather and parchment are made from animal skin, stripped and dried, then cut into sections. Each person involved in the processing of these materials somehow influences them, however subtly. For this reason, much greater care must be taken to thoroughly banish all traces of previous existence from the materials used to make talismans.

The reasons for carrying talismans are usually of a more specific nature than amulets. In fact, there are literally thousands of different kinds of talismans presented in various published grimoires, each used for some specific purpose. In the third section of *The Book of the Sacred Magic of Abra-melin, the Mage*, translated by S. L. MacGregor-Mathers in 1883,[12] there are approximately 250 talismans illustrated, each with a specific purpose ranging from "to transform Men into Asses," to "to take on the appearance of an Old Woman." In *The Key of Solomon*, also translated by Mathers, there are described forty-four talismans which were to be consecrated to the planetary forces, and are for purposes ranging from "exciting earthquakes" to "the operation of invisibility." See figure 27. Additionally, *The Goetia*, or *Lesser Key of Solomon*, translated by Aleister Crowley in 1903, includes 72 talismans, each used to control a specific "evil spirit." Performing acts from these ancient Hebrew grimoires is not recommended, unless all preliminaries described can be fulfilled, much of which may well prove next to impossible. To illustrate, the following is from Book II, chapter XVII of the *Key of Solomon*:

---

[12]Which was originally translated from the Hebrew in 1458. It should also be noted that any operation outlined in the *Book of Abra-Melin* requires the practitioner to prepare for a period of more than six months, performing certain rituals and following daily regiments of various procedures, all of which is thoroughly detailed in the text. This preparation period is essential, as explained in the text, to the success of any operation detailed therein.

Virgin parchment is necessary in many Magical Operations, and should be properly prepared and consecrated. There are two kinds, one called Virgin, the other Unborn. Virgin parchment is that which is taken from an Animal which hath not attained the age of generation, whether it be ram, kid, or other animal.

Unborn parchment is taken from an animal which hath been taken before its time from the uterus of its mother.

Take whichsoever of these two classes of animals thou pleasest, provided only that it be male, and in the day and hour of Mercury; and take it to a secret place where no man may see thee at work. Thou shalt have a marsh-reed cut at a single stroke with a new knife, and thou shalt strip from it the leaves, repeating this Conjuration:

THE CONJURATION OF THE REED

I conjure thee by the Creator of all things, and by the King of Angels, Whose Name is EL SHADDAI, that thou receivest strength and virtue to flay this animal and to construct the parchment whereon I may write the Holy Names of God, and that it may acquire so great virtue that all which I shall write or do may obtain its effect, through Him who liveth unto the Eternal Ages. Amen.

Before cutting the Reed recite Psalm lxxii.

After this, with the Knife of the Art, thou shalt fashion the Reed into the shape of a knife, and upon it thou shalt write these Names: AGLA, ADONAI, ELOHI, through Whom be the work of this Knife accomplished. Then thou shalt say:

O God, Who drewest Moses, Thy well beloved and Thine elect, from among the Reeds on the marshy banks of the Nile, and from the Waters, he being yet a child, grant unto me through Thy great mercy and compassion that this Reed may recieve Power and Virtue to effect that which I desire through Thy Holy Name and the Names of Thy Holy Angels. Amen.

This being done, thou shalt commence with this Knife to flay the Animal, whether it be Virgin or Unborn, saying . . .[13]

Several more conjurations and instructions follow, leading into a three day drying procedure; but needless to say, this operation requires procedures that would be most difficult to accomplish in the 20th century. Unless these complicated specifications are followed as formally detailed, the operation attempted will be doomed for failure, and could conceivably result in tragedy.[14]

Since a well-rounded magician should be capable of constructing and properly charging talismans, it is recommended that the novice practitioner begin with a basic

---

[13]*The Key of Solomon the King*, pp. 111–112.

[14]It should be noted that I have no question regarding the effectiveness of the magickal operations outlined in these extremely reputable grimoires, when properly performed; for I have seen and performed many such operations, precisely as detailed, and been witness to both successful results, as well as disastrous failures. The main problem with performing operations from ancient grimoires stems from the inconsistencies and errors which naturally occur after multiple translations, as well as the fact that it was common practice for the writers of the original texts to occasionally leave out, or conceal vital details required for the complete fulfillment of the operation. This information would then be handed down by word of mouth, or on separate pages as a "key" to the system

Table 4. Elemental and Planetary Talisman Construction.

TALISMAN	DISK COLOR	SIGIL COLOR	HEBREW LETTERS	SIGIL
Earth	Black	Yellow	אנלא	▽
Water	Olive	Yellow	אהיה	▽
Air	Citrine	Yellow	יהוה	△
Fire	Russet	Yellow	ארני	△
Lunar	Violet	Indigo	שרי אל חי	☽
Mercurial	Orange	Violet-purple	אלהים צכאות	☿
Venutian	Emerald	Amber	יהוה צכאות	♀
Solar	Yellow	Pink-rose	יהוה אלוה ודעת	☉
Martian	Scarlet	Orange	אלהים נגוד	♂
Jupiterian	Blue	Violet	אל	♃

qabalistic talismanic system. This system utilizes small wooden disks, which can be found in most arts and crafts stores. The student will be required to construct a total of eleven talismans, four of which will be elemental talismans, and seven will be planetary talismans. These particular talismans will be of a general nature, rather than a specific one.

Before constructing these talismans, you should first acquire all eleven wooden disks, each of the paint colors listed in Table 4, and a bottle of clear finish. Also needed will be two paintbrushes; one medium brush to efficiently paint the disk a single color, and another for the fine lettering and sigils. Each of these objects, including each bottle of paint, must be banished, purified and consecrated immediately upon acquiring them. This should be done in one ritual, which will likely take a full hour to complete, and is outlined here:

1) The circle should be prepared as in Step 1-A of "A

Lunar Invocation." The altar should be prepared in advance, with setup as follows:

- The censer in the east, using Abramelin Incense.
- A vial of Abramelin Oil in the south.
- A bowl of hyssop-treated, natural water in the west.
- A dish of natural salt in the north.
- All disks, paints, finish and brushes in the center.

2) The magician should first take the ritual bath in hyssop-treated water, speaking the words of purification at some time while bathing.

3) After bathing, and before entering the circle area, the magician should make the mark of the Rose Cross over his or her heart in Abramelin Oil, while speaking the words of consecration.

4) Then don the robe, and enter the circle area, moving to the west side of the altar, facing east.

5) Perform the Lesser Banishing Ritual of the Pentagram, and then the Lesser Banishing Ritual of the Hexagram.

6) From the west side of the altar, pick up the first disk in your left hand, dip your right forefinger into the bowl of water, and sprinkle the disk with a drop or two while saying, "Asperges me, EHIEH (vibrate), Hyssoppo et mundabor. Lavabis me et super nivem dealbabor."

7) Still holding the disk in your left hand, move deosil to the east side of the altar, and hold the disk over the censer in the incense's smoke, while saying, "Of pure will, unassuaged of purpose, in every way perfect." [Aleister Crowley, *Book of the Law*, 1904] Then vibrate YEHUWAU.

8) Still holding the disk in your left hand, move deosil to the south side of the altar, dab a bit of Abramelin Oil on your finger and touch it to the disk while saying, "Accendat in nobis ADONAI [vibrate] ignem sui amoris et flammam aeternae caritatis."

9) Still holding the disk in your left hand, move deosil to the north side of the altar, dab a bit of salt on your finger and touch it to the disk while saying, "I am uplifted in thine heart, and the kisses of the stars rain hard upon my body." [Aleister Crowley, *Book of the Law*, 1904.] Then vibrate AGLA.

10) Move deosil back to the west side of the altar, facing east, and replace the disk to the center of the altar. Perform this same procedure with every item individually. Use the outside of the paint bottles, except when in the south. There introduce a single drop of Abramelin Oil in each bottle, while speaking the words of consecration. [If the paint is not purchased in glass bottles, place it in such before the ritual.]

11) After completing the process with each item, perform the Lesser Banishing Ritual of the Pentagram and the Lesser Banishing Ritual of the Hexagram. Then hold your dagger above your head and say, "And now I say unto thee, depart in peace unto thine habitations and abodes—and may the blessings of the highest be upon thee in the name of (vibrate) YEHUWAU, and let there be peace between thee and me; and be thou very ready to come, whensoever thou art invoked and called, either by a word, or by a will or by this mighty conjuration of Magick Art." Then strike the altar top once with the butt of the dagger, and say "I now declare this temple duly closed." The materials are now prepared to make talismans from. [At this point, it should be needless to mention that all rituals, details and events should be extensively and thoroughly documented in one's magickal records.]

The four elemental talismans may be constructed and charged as a group; however, each of the planetary talismans should be constructed and charged individually.

Begin by constructing the earth talisman. This should be painted completely black, and after the paint dries, then the Hebrew letters AGLA (from right to left, aleph, gimel, lamed, aleph) should be painted in the upper portion of the talisman in yellow. Beneath these letters should be painted the elemental sign of earth, also in yellow paint (as depicted in Table 4). After the paint dries, a coat of clear finish should be applied. When that dries, the talisman should be wrapped in a piece of black silk, and concealed in a secluded place. The water, air, and fire talismans should be painted according to Table 4, and then treated as the earth talisman.

These four talismans should be left undisturbed for a period of no less than thirty days, before performing the charging ritual. Also, these four should be constructed and charged before beginning to construct the planetary talismans.

The following is the charging ritual for the elemental talismans:

1) The circle should be prepared as in Step 1-A of "A Lunar Invocation." The altar should be prepared in advance, with setup as follows:

• A single white candle should be placed in the east, north, west and south.

• Each magickal weapon should be atop the altar in its respective direction.

• The censer in the east, using Abramelin incense.

• A vial of Abramelin Oil in the south.

• A bowl of hyssop-treated, natural water in the west.

• A dish of natural salt in the north.

• The four disks should be placed in the center.

2) The magician should first take the ritual bath in hyssop-treated water, speaking the words of purification at some time while bathing.

3) After bathing, and before entering the circle area, the magician should make the mark of the Rose Cross over his or her heart in Abramelin Oil, while speaking the words of consecration.

4) Then don the robe, and enter the circle area, moving to the west side of the altar, facing east.

5) Perform the Banishing Ritual of the Serpent.

6) From the west side of the altar, pick up the earth disk in your left hand, dip your right forefinger into the bowl of water and sprinkle the disk with a drop or two while saying, "Asperges me, EHIEH (vibrate), Hyssoppo et mundabor. Lavabis me et super nivem dealbabor."

7) Still holding the disk in your left hand, move deosil to the east side of the altar and hold the disk over the censer in the incense's smoke, while saying "Of pure will, unassuaged of purpose, in every way perfect," and then vibrate YEHUWAU.

8) Still holding the disk in your left hand, move deosil to the south side of the altar, dab a bit of Abramelin Oil on your finger and touch it to the disk while saying, "Accendat in nobis ADONAI (vibrate) ignem sui amoris et flammam aeternae caritatis."

9) Still holding the disk in your left hand, move deosil to the north side of the altar, dab a bit of salt on your finger and touch it to the disk while saying, "I am uplifted in thine

heart, and the kisses of the stars rain hard upon my body," and then vibrate AGLA.

10) Place the earth disk next to the salt dish on the north side of the altar, and return moving deosil to the west side of the altar, facing east.

11) Repeat Steps 6 through 10 with the water talisman next, and then place it next to the water bowl, on the west side of the altar.

12) Repeat Steps 6 through 10 with the air talisman, placing it on the east side of the altar, next to the censer.

13) Repeat Steps 6 through 10 with the fire talisman, placing it on the south side of the altar, next to the vial of oil.

14) Move deosil back to the west side of the altar facing east.

15) Now walk around the altar to your left, and move to the easternmost point of the circle. Make a sharp right turn and circumambulate deosil for ten revolutions, making the "Sign of Horus" or "The Enterer" in the east, as described in Step 8 of "A Lunar Invocation" in chapter 12. Stop after the tenth circumambulation and return (always moving deosil) to the west side of the altar, facing east.

16) Now clap your hands loudly in two batteries of three, divided by one battery of four. [Clap 3 times, then clap 4 times, then clap 3 times.]

17) Then, move to the north side of the altar, pick up the ritual disk with your right hand, and face the north. With the disk, make the invoking pentagram of the equilibrium of passives [figure 7, page 33] while vibrating AGLA. Atop that pentagram, make the invoking pentagram of earth while vibrating ADONAI.

18) Quickly return the disk to its place on the altar, and pick up the earth talisman. With both hands, hold the talisman in the center of the pentagrams which you just made, and vibrate AGLA. You should barely detect a cold, dry, sensation emanating from the north, and see a brown-greenish aura surrounding the talisman. Leave it in place for thirty seconds or so, before returning it to the north side of the altar.

19) As it sits on the altar, lift the northern candle up and allow a few drops of wax from the candle to fall on the talisman. This is symbolically "sealing" the energy in the talisman. This talisman is now charged.

20) Move deosil to the west side of the altar, pick up the ritual cup in your right hand, and face the west. With the cup, make the invoking pentagram of the equilibrium of passives while vibrating AGLA. Atop that pentagram, make the invoking pentagram of water while vibrating EL.

21) Quickly return the cup to its place on the altar, and pick up the water talisman. With both hands, hold the talisman in the center of the pentagrams, and vibrate EHIEH. You should notice a cool, moist, sensation, and see a bluish aura surrounding the talisman. Leave it in place for thirty seconds, before returning it to the west side of the altar.

22) As it sits on the altar, lift the western candle up and allow a few drops of wax from the candle to fall on the talisman.

23) Move deosil to the east side of the altar, pick up the ritual dagger in your right hand, and face the east. With the dagger, make the invoking pentagrams of the equilibrium of actives, while vibrating EHIEH. Atop that pentagram, make the invoking pentagram of air while vibrating YEHUWAU.

24) Quickly return the dagger to its place on the altar, and pick up the air talisman. With both hands, hold the talisman in the center of the pentagrams, and vibrate YEHUWAU. You should feel a warm, moist, sensation, and the aura should be yellowish. Leave it in place for thirty seconds, before returning it to the altar.

25) As it sits on the altar, lift the eastern candle up and allow a few drops of wax from the candle to fall on the talisman.

26) Move deosil to the south side of the altar, pick up the ritual wand in your right hand, and face the south. With the wand make the invoking pentagram of the equilibrium of actives, while vibrating EHIEH. Atop that pentagram, make the invoking pentagram of fire, while vibrating ELOHIM.

27) Quickly return the wand to its place, and pick up the fire talisman. With both hands, hold it in the center of the pentagrams, while vibrating ADONAI. You should feel a hot, dry, sensation, and see a reddish aura around the talisman. After thirty seconds, return it to its place on the altar.

28) As it sits on the altar, lift the southern candle up and allow a few drops of wax from the candle to fall on the talisman. All four elemental talismans are now properly charged.

29) Moving deosil, return to the west side of the altar, facing east, and extinguish the four candles.

30) Perform the Banishing Ritual of the Serpent.

31) Hold your dagger above your head and say "And now I say unto thee, depart in peace unto thine habitations and abodes—and may the blessings of the highest be upon thee in the name of (vibrate) ADONAI MELECH, and let there

be peace between thee and me; and be thou very ready to come, whensoever thou art invoked and called, either by a word, or by a will or by this mighty conjuration of Magick Art." Then with the butt of the dagger, strike the top of the altar ten times. First 3 times, pause, then 4 times, pause, then 3 times, and say, "I now declare this temple duly closed." Then strike the altar once.

After the four elemental talismans are charged, they should be wrapped in silk cloth corresponding to their elemental colors (as are the elemental weapons).

The next talisman constructed should be the lunar one. This should be painted violet, with the Hebrew letters ShDI AL ChI above the lunar sigil, both painted in indigo (see Table 4, page 160). After drying, this should be kept concealed in a black silk cloth for a period of no less than thirty days. The following charging ritual should be performed on a Monday.

1) Follow Steps 1 through 10 of the last ritual. The only difference should be that there is only the lunar talisman in the center, and also a single indigo candle in the center of the altar, besides the four white candles in each direction.

2) Move deosil back to the west side of the altar, facing east.

3) Now walk around the altar to your left and move to the easternmost point of the circle. Make a sharp right turn and circumambulate deosil for nine revolutions, making the sign of Horus or The Enterer in the east. Stop after the ninth circumambulation and return (always moving deosil) to the west side of the altar, facing east.

4) Now clap your hands loudly in three batteries of three.

5) Using the wand, make the invoking lunar hexagram above the altar, while vibrating ARARITA.

6) Quickly return the wand to its place on the altar, and pick up the lunar talisman. With both hands, hold it in the center of the hexagram while vibrating SHADAI EL CHAI. There should be an indigo aura surrounding the talisman. Hold it in place for at least thirty seconds, before returning it to the center of the altar.

7) Then pick up the indigo candle, and allow a few drops of wax from the candle to fall on the talisman. This talisman is now charged.

8) You should be facing the east still, on the west side of the altar. Now extinguish first the center candle, and then the four white candles.

9) Perform the Banishing Ritual of the Serpent.

10) Hold your dagger above your head and say, "And now I say unto thee, depart in peace unto thine habitations and abodes—and may the blessings of the highest be upon thee in the name of (vibrate) SHADAI EL CHAI, and let there be peace between thee and me; and be thou very ready to come, whensoever thou art invoked and called, either by a word, or by a will or by this mighty conjuration of Magick Art." Then with the butt of the dagger, strike the top of the altar ten times. First 3 times, pause, then 4 times, pause, then 3 times, and say, "I now declare this temple duly closed." Then strike the altar once.

After charging the lunar talisman, it should be wrapped in an indigo-colored silk cloth, and concealed in a secluded place.

You may then begin work on the Mercurial talisman, which should be painted orange, with the Hebrew letters and sigil painted in violet-purple (See Table 4, page 160.) It should also be wrapped in a black silk cloth, and left concealed for no less than thirty days.

The ritual for charging this talisman is identical to the last ritual, except for the following substitutions. The ritual should be performed on a Wednesday. There should be a violet-purple candle next to the talisman, in the center of the altar. There should be eight circumambulations, and the clapping in Step 4 should be in two batteries of three, divided by one battery of two. The wand should be used again, but using the invoking hexagram of Mercury, and vibrating ELOHIM TZBAOTH. The aura should be a violet-purple, and the closing God-name to be vibrated is ELOHIM TZBAOTH. The charged talisman should be placed in violet-purple silk, and then concealed.

You may then begin work on the Venutian talisman, which should be painted emerald-green, with the Hebrew letters and sigil painted in amber. It should also be wrapped in a black silk cloth, and left concealed for no less than thirty days.

The ritual for charging this talisman is identical to the last ritual, except for the following substitutions. The ritual should be performed on a Friday. There should be an amber candle next to the talisman, in the center of the altar. There should be seven circumambulations, and the clapping in Step 4 should be in two batteries of two, divided by one battery of three. The wand should be used again, but using the invoking hexagram of Venus, and vibrating YEHUWAU TZBAOTH. The aura should be an amber color, and the closing God-name to be vibrated is YEHUWAU TZBAOTH. The charged talisman should be placed in amber colored silk, and then concealed.

You may then begin work on the Solar talisman, which should be painted yellow, with the Hebrew letters and sigil painted in a pink-rose. It should also be wrapped in a black silk cloth, and left concealed for no less than thirty days.

The ritual for charging this talisman is identical to the last ritual, except for the following substitutions. The ritual should be performed on a Sunday. There should be a pink-rose candle next to the talisman, in the center of the altar. There should be six circumambulations, and the clapping in Step 4 should be in three batteries of two. The wand should be used again, but using the invoking Solar hexagram, and vibrating YEHUWAU ALOAH VEDOTH. The aura should be a pink-rose color, and the closing God-name to be vibrated is YEHUWAU ALOAH VEDOTH. The charged talisman should be wrapped in rose-pink colored silk, and then concealed.

You may then begin work on the Martian talisman, which should be painted scarlet-red, with the Hebrew letters and sigil painted in orange. It should also be wrapped in a black silk cloth, and left concealed for no less than thirty days.

The ritual for charging this talisman is identical to the last ritual, except for the following substitutions. The ritual should be performed on a Tuesday. There should be an orange candle next to the talisman, in the center of the altar. There should be five circumambulations, and the clapping in Step 4 should be in two batteries of two, divided by a single clap. The wand should be used again, but using the invoking hexagram of Mars, and vibrating ELOHIM GIBOR. The aura should be an orange color, and the closing God-name to be vibrated is ELOHIM GIBOR. The charged talisman should be wrapped in orange colored silk, and then concealed.

Finally, you may then begin work on the Jupiterian talisman, which should be painted blue, with the Hebrew letters and sigil painted in violet. It should also be wrapped in a black silk cloth, and left concealed for no less than thirty days.

The ritual for charging this talisman is identical to the last ritual, except for the following substitutions. The ritual should be performed on a Thursday. There should be a violet candle next to the talisman, in the center of the altar. There should be four circumambulations, and the clapping in Step 4 should be in two batteries of one, divided by one battery of two. The wand should be used again, but using the invoking hexagram of Jupiter, and vibrating EL. The aura should be a violet color, and the closing God-name to be vibrated is EL. The charged talisman should be wrapped in violet colored silk, and then concealed.[15]

This being accomplished, the student is well equipped with a full armory of talismans. They should all be kept wrapped in their individual silk cloth, and if carried, should be wrapped in silk, within a leather pouch. They should never be removed from their cloths, except to recharge them, which should be done four times yearly for each one. The wax should be gently, but completely, cleaned off before recharging them. Additionally, if any speck of the wax seal happens to come loose, for any reason, the talisman must be cleaned of wax, and recharged.

These talismans are of a general nature, rather than the specific nature of those mentioned earlier. They are talismans of the "highest" magick, not meant to produce results on the "lower" or material planes. They are to be used when you feel yourself "lacking" of a certain quality. They each contain energy of a specific force, with a specific quality, and can be carried separately or in combination.[16] If you believe yourself to be lacking in Mercurial qualities, for instance, you should carry the Mercurial talisman. If you feel that the books being studied are too difficult to digest, the Mercurial talisman should be carried while studying. If you are seeking companionship or love, the Venutian talisman should be carried. If you wish to acquire material gain, financially or otherwise, then you should carry the earth talisman.

Although these talismans are not of a specific nature, this system of talismanic magic should inspire resourceful

---

[15]It should be needless to say that all pieces of silk should be purified and consecrated individually, as you would do to any and all magickal implements.

[16]But never should two be wrapped in the same cloth.

students to experiment with the system, ultimately devising their own. Students may wish to devise a talisman for a specific purpose. They would then determine which planetary force best represents this purpose. After developing a working knowledge of the Qabalah, they will realize that the ultimate result of any operation may be classified tentatively in one of the following categories:

1) Elemental: for works which cause results on the material plane;

- Earth: for material gain, to acquire a particular object;

- Water: for grace and beauty;

- Air: for swift motion;

- Fire: for intensity of impression.

2) Lunar: for works of illusion, enchantment, for travel, reconcilation, acquiring visions.

3) Mercurial: to acquire wisdom, or to grasp intellectual matter, also for business, eloquence, arts and sciences, predictions.

4) Venutian: to sharpen instinctive ability; also for love, friendliness, companionship, kindness, pleasure.

5) Solar: to advance spiritually.

6) Martian and Jupiterian talismans should not be constructed for specific purposes, although advanced students will know the manner in which to do so.

The Order of the Golden Dawn, a traditional magickal order, has devised several extremely effective modern talismanic systems. These are outlined in Volume 5 of *The Complete Golden Dawn System of Magic*, edited by Israel

Regardie.[17] Students should make a study of this book. The Golden Dawn has developed groundbreaking material in various magickal subjects. Many past students of this Order are leading occult figures today, such as Aleister Crowley. But specifically, Volume 5 entails excellent systems of talismanic magic, which may be easily incorporated with the Qabalistic system outlined here.

This discussion will close with the suggestion that you develop your own system of qabalistic talismanic magic, as this is what the great magicians of the past—such as Solomon and Abramelin—have done. These systems are not to be imitated, rather they are examples of the manner in which your own system should be constructed.

---

[17]Israel Regardie, *The Complete Golden Dawn System of Magic* (Phoenix, AZ: New Falcon), 1991.

CHAPTER 16

A VENUTIAN INVOCATION

The following is an invocation of Venus, which, when properly performed, greatly improves your natural and instinctive abilities, and inspires the human spirit with the forces of Love. This invocation should be performed whenever Venus' orbit brings it close to Earth.

1) Prepare the temple:

• Prepare the circle as in Step 1-A of "A Lunar Invocation" in chapter 12.

• Paint a seven-pointed star in the circle. This should be painted amber, and the tips of the star should just touch the inner border of the circle.

• One emerald-green candle should be placed at the tip of each point of the star, and within the inner and outer borders of the circle.

• Arrange the altar in the center of the circle, with the front of it facing east.

• Arrange four white candles on top of the altar, in each of the four directions.

• Next to each candle on the altar should be the appropriate magickal weapon.

• Place a vial of oil next to the candle in the south, a vial of natural water next to the candle in the west, a dish of natural salt next to the candle in the north, and the censer next to the candle in the east.

- Benzoin or rose incense should be used.

2) Prepare yourself:

- You should have been performing each of the rituals outlined in chapter 4 daily, and also meditating daily, for several months previous to the performance of this ritual.

- Study pictures or statues of all the Venutian gods, such as Venus, Aphrodite and Hathoor, until their images are firmly fixed in your mind. Also, read any information regarding them you can find in books on mythological figures, etc.

- The best time to perform this particular invocation is at a time when Venus is visible in the evening sky.

- After preparing the temple, wait until approximately thirty minutes before the designated time for the beginning of the ritual, and then take a nice long bath using water that has been treated with hyssop and a few drops of rose or Abramelin Oil. Relax and clear your mind. Allow all thoughts to flow away with the water. Several times during the bathing, speak the words of consecration.

- After the bathing, consecrate yourself with Abramelin Oil. Use your right forefinger to make the sign of the Rose Cross over your heart, while speaking the words of consecration.

- Now clear your mind in meditation for a few minutes, then put on your robe, and the venutian amulet, which was described in chapter 15. You are now ready to move to the circle area, and begin the invocation.

3) Perform the Banishing Ritual of the Serpent.

4) After the banishing, move to the west side of the altar facing the east. Then move deosil around the altar, to the south. Light the white candle there and moving deosil, light

the other three. Then return to the west side of altar, facing east.

5) Move deosil to the east side of the altar and light the incense in the censer. Then move to the easternmost emerald candle and light it. Moving deosil, light the other six candles around the circle, and then move back to the west side of the altar, facing east.

6) With the butt of the dagger, strike the altar once and state, "I am (your name and grades, if any)."

7) State the oath: "Hear me and know that I am now going to invoke the spirit and power of VENUS, so I may obtain the Vision of Beauty Triumphant, learn of the forces of Love, and improve my perceptions of the mysteries of nature. I will not leave this circle until I succeed in this operation because it is necessary for me to progress in my spiritual attainment!" Then, knock once with the butt of the dagger on the altar.

8) Now walk around the altar to your left and move to the easternmost point of the circle. Make a sharp right turn and circumambulate deosil seven times, making the sign of Horus or The Enterer in the east. Stop after the seventh circumambulation and return deosil to the west side of the altar, facing east.

9) Pick up the wand in your right hand and the cup in your left. Hold them over head and knock them together seven times in two batteries of two, divided by one of three (knock 2 times, pause, knock 3 times, pause and knock 2 times). Then begin the conjurations:

[At this point, the magician should assume the God-form of Hathoor, as described in Appendix B, and maintain that form through Step 10.]

As I weave this mystic spell 'neath the sky of a starry
    night,
    vaporous clouds unveil an orb of the palest white.
Beaming down with inspiration;
    exhalted in my adoration;
engulfing this circle in an emerald light.
      VENUS, I invoke thee!
Descend and inspire me.

Hear me Venus, Aphrodite;
    for the currents carry my words on high
upward to that mighty palace, where the Gods
    reside.
I call on the divine essence of Netzach, grace me with
    your presence,
and embrace me as our two worlds collide.
      VENUS, I invoke thee!
Descend and inspire me.

Desire invokes the apparition, never changing o'er the
    years;
    and then the enchanting vision
of beauty triumphant appears.
    Before unsuspecting eyes, a beautiful naked
    woman cries,
while bloodstained roses await her tears.
      VENUS, I invoke thee!
Descend and inspire me.

A dazzling image takes form, robed in silken amber
    flesh.
    So vibrantly soft and warm, every touch a sensual
    caress;
in motion, seductively erotic;
    her scent, enticingly exotic;
my heart and soul, she doth now possess.
      VENUS, I invoke thee!
Descend and inspire me.

10) Then, with your wand, make the Invoking Hexagram of Venus overhead while vibrating "ARARITA." Then touch the wand to the center of the hexagram and vibrate "YEHUWAU TZBAOTH." Then, the forces of Venus shall fill your circle and completely envelop everything in the confines with lunar energy. Bask in the power and absorb all the energy that flows toward you.

11) Closing the temple:

• When the time is right, rise (if you are sitting) and extinquish the emerald-green candles, starting in the east and moving widdershins; and then, still moving widdershins, return to the west side of the altar and face east.

• Perform the Banishing Ritual of the Serpent.

• Hold your dagger above your head and say, "And now I say unto thee, depart in peace unto thine habitations and abodes—and may the blessings of the highest be upon thee in the name of (vibrate) ARARITA—YEHUWAU TZBAOTH, and let there be peace between thee and me; and be thou very ready to come, whensoever thou art invoked and called, either by a word, or by a will or by this mighty conjuration of Magick Art."

• Then with the butt of the dagger, strike the top of the altar ten times. First 3 times, pause, then 4 times, pause, then 3 times, and say, "I now declare this temple duly closed." Then strike the altar once.

CHAPTER 17

THE TAROT

One of the most popular methods of divination used today is a system which employs what appears to be a deck of playing cards, and is most commonly referred to as the tarot. There are many different types of tarot decks in existence, and they can be found in many thousands of homes all over the world; but for all who possess the tarot, few are aware of its actual primary purpose. The fact that it is an excellent system of divination masks the most useful and important aspect of this powerful tool of the highest magick.

There is so much speculation regarding the origin of the tarot, and very little documented evidence of its early existence, that we need not bother attempting to describe its possible history; except to say that most agree the first recorded use of the tarot dates from the 14th century in the general area of the Mediterranean Sea. Many early decks are of Italian or French origin.

The qabalistic symbolism of the tarot is too significant to ignore. The relationship between the 78 cards of the tarot and the Tree of Life glyph is undeniable. Additionally, the 22 trump cards are simply too well-suited to the 22 paths of the Tree to be entirely coincidental. Another possibly coincidental relationship was the publication of ancient qabalistic material, being released to the world during the 14th century, in the form of the controversial printing of The Zohar by Moses De Leon of Spain. This was allegedly translated from ancient manuscripts of Simeon Ben Yochai, and is said to date back to the second century of the Common Era. There have been several questions raised regarding the

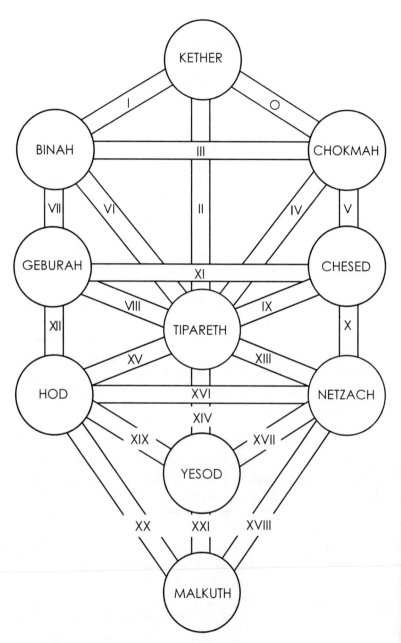

Figure 28. The Tarot Trumps on the Tree of Life.

validity of these manuscripts, although no evidence ever proved them to be either forgeries or authentic. There has never been any question about their qabalistic value, however; so rather than wasting energy debating unknowns, we would find our time better spent comparing the Tree of Life glyph to the tarot system.[1] See figure 28).

1) As stated earlier, the 22 trump cards fit perfectly into the paths of the Tree, and are in fact, primary symbols of the paths on the modern tree. [See 777.]

2) The 40 "number" cards (ace through ten of the four suits—wands, cups, swords and disks) represent the ten sephiroth in each of the four elemental worlds, as outlined here:

- Wands represent Atziluth, world of Emanations, fire.

- Swords represent Briah, world of Creation, air.

- Cups represent Yetzirah, world of Formation, water.

- Disks represent Assiah, world of Manifestation, earth.

The number of the card corresponds to the number of a given sephiroth (Ace = Kether, Two = Chokmah, Three = Binah, etc.).

3) The remaining sixteen "royal face" cards are commonly described as being related to certain sephiroth on the Tree (Knights to Chokmah, Queens to Binah, Princes to Tiphareth, and Princesses to Malkuth) but a lesser-known theory dealing with these cards better represents symmetry within the Tree. This theory states that every "royal face" card describes some outer influence of a particular nature. To be more specific, a secondary elemental force within its own elemental

---

[1] I suspect that the tarot was derived from, and is an integral offshoot of, the Tree of Life, possibly an ancient attempt to educate the common people to the mystical system of qabala by use of a learning game.

world. (These could be considered "sub-elements.") Each of these cards is an individual representation of the four worlds within each of the four worlds. The Knights symbolize fiery aspects, Queens symbolize watery aspects, Princes symbolize airy aspects, and the Princesses symbolize earthy aspects. (For example, the Prince of Cups represents the airy nature of water, the Queen of Disks represents the watery nature of earth, etc.) These outer influences are almost always some unknown and higher force, and our knowledge of these influences will not change them. So depending on the situation, it becomes necessary to adapt in order to allow the force to assist rather than hinder.

For divination purposes, it's best not to learn how to read the cards by practice at first. To arbitrarily read layouts straight out of some "generic" type book on the tarot, with some other person's interpretations of the cards, is a valueless exercise. The explanatory tarot guides, such as A. E. Waite's *Pictorial Key to the Tarot*, or *The Tarot Revealed*, by Eden Gray, are valuable collections for study; but to accurately read the cards requires your own individual interpretation of every card to be fixed in your mind. Since every person sees the cards somehow differently, serious tarot students must spend a good deal of time getting to know the cards. Handle them, shuffle them, examine and study them. Listen to what they may tell you.

To become adept with the tarot, it is necessary to create a notebook of the meanings of every card as they relate to you.[2] This is best done in a three part system which is outlined below. You can also study the explanations that accompany the deck you buy, as they are the author's or artist's interpretations of the cards. This will give you an idea of their influences and impressions of their own work.

---

[2]The cards tend to stimulate some kind of a reaction in a person, and this reaction varies in different people; in much the same way as a cat might stimulate love in some people, and hate or fear in others.

1) First, separate all the trump cards from the deck, and shuffle them for several minutes, while clearing your mind as if preparing to meditate.

2) At random, lay out five cards face down in front of you. Then sit for several minutes and completely blank out your mind before picking up the first card. Glance quickly at it and then record the very first thoughts that enter your mind. Do you like or dislike it? Does it interest you or bore you? Do you register warmth, fear, coldness, happiness? Any and every feeling should be noted. After recording everything, set the card back down, and clear your mind once again for several minutes before proceeding with the next card. After following this procedure with all five cards, move on to Step 3.

3) With the same five cards face down in front of you, once again clear your mind before picking up the first card. This time, study it for at least five or six minutes. Examine every detail about it, and then record a description and your impressions of the symbolisms contained in it. What does it mean to you? How do you feel about this card? Does it symbolize success, pleasure, hate, loneliness, despair, strength, weakness, or indifference? Any and every impression, no matter how apparently trivial, should be recorded. After noting all impressions, replace the card face down in its place, clear your mind once again before proceeding to the next card, and then repeat the procedure. After you have read all five cards, move on to Step 4. [It may be advisable to complete the first two steps with all 22 trump cards (called the major arcana) before moving on to Step 4. Use your own judgment.]

4) Sitting with the cards face down in front of you, clear your mind completely for several minutes and pick up the first card. Gaze casually at it, not specifically noting any details. Attempt to take in the scene as a whole for about

half a minute or so, and then try to decide what you think the card is trying to say to you. Tell yourself that this card is trying to tell you something, and open up your mind so that you can listen. Record all the ideas and results that you receive. [Take at least a twenty-minute break between cards.]

Follow this three-step procedure with each of the four suits after you have completed interpretations on the trumps. The notebook you begin should be expanded regularly. A separate page should be kept for each of the 78 cards, although it is not necessary to fill that page on the first few experiments. You should continue to repeat this procedure on a monthly or semi-monthly basis, until you can easily recognize the appropriate interpretation of every card when randomly drawn. This may require years of study, and over time, several pages should be devoted to each card. Never should outdated interpretations be erased or discarded. Just date any updated information and notations, so you may evaluate your own progress.

As I mentioned briefly in an earlier paragraph, the tarot is more than simply a technique of divination. That is merely one of several secondary uses of the cards. Actually, the tarot is a powerful tool of "self" communication; it is a medium between your mind and that hidden, yet ever-present, spirit and guiding light that every person individually possesses. With the tarot, you open the gate for that secret part of yourself to express its knowledge of your life, either to advise or just to communicate, without having to reveal its presence.

The drawback that accompanies this theory is that it contradicts the assumption that some "outer force" guides the hand of the card reader; but since that force is actually your inner self (for who better to guide your hand than your own "self"), you would only obtain accurate readings when casting your own cards. To read someone else's cards puts you in that person's place, hence the reading would reflect your own influences and judgments in the situation that the other person finds him- or herself in. Your cards would express what would be appropriate for you under the given circumstances, and being that every person is a "star" —somehow different, and on an individual path—it could be highly probable that what would be right for you could easily be wrong for someone else.

The tarot is often referred to as "fortune telling cards," and it is said that you can "read the future" with them.[3] It's true that, with a good working knowledge, you may obtain accurate information regarding future events; however, another useful aspect of the cards is that you can learn about your past. This does not refer to the past years of your current life. Rather, the tarot is capable of shedding some light on your past lives, for the inner self you communicate with through the cards has lived all of those lives, and is in fact, your proverbial immortal spirit, otherwise known as the eternal soul.

In my opinion, the tarot is ultimately a sophisticated tool of communication between an individual and his or her inner self. With the proper application, the cards serve as keys to that treasure-house of memories and experiences that one has collected for as long as he or she has existed. There one can tap into the knowledge of previous lives, as well as gaining insight into future occurrences. If one so desires, the tarot allows one to learn all that one has ever been, and all that one will ever be. To "know thyself" is one of the most important goals of the ritual magician.

---

[3]Which is not technically the same as "divination," or to divine information from.

CHAPTER 18

A SOLAR INVOCATION

The following is a Solar Invocation, which, when properly performed, greatly improves your ability to spiritually advance. It illuminates you with the forces of light and beauty. This invocation should be performed on a monthly basis, on the day of the new moon.

1) Prepare the temple:

• Prepare the circle as in Step 1-A of "A Lunar Invocation" in chapter 12.

• Paint a six-pointed star in the circle. This should be painted pink-rose, and the tips of the star should just touch the inner border of the circle.

• One yellow candle should be placed at the tip of each point of the star, and within the inner and outer borders of the circle.

• Arrange the altar in the center of the circle, with the front of it facing east.

• Arrange four white candles on top of the altar, in each of the four directions.

• Next to each candle on the altar should be the appropriate magickal weapon.

• Place a vial of oil next to the candle in the south, a vial of natural water next to the candle in the west, a dish of natural salt next to the candle in the north, and the censer next to the candle in the east.

• Use frankincense or Abramelin incense.

2) Prepare yourself:

• You should have been performing each of the rituals outlined in chapter 4 daily, and also meditating daily, for several months previous to the performance of this ritual.

• Study pictures or statues of all the Solar gods, such as Apollo, Iacchus and Ra, until their images are firmly fixed in your mind. Also, read any information regarding them you can find in books on mythological figures, etc.

• The best time to perform this particular invocation is at twelve o'clock noon, preferably on a clear day.

• After preparing the temple, wait until approximately thirty minutes before the designated time for the beginning of the ritual, and then take a nice long bath using water that has been treated with hyssop and a few drops of frankincense oil [Abramelin Oil is also suitable]. Relax and clear your mind. Allow all thoughts to flow away with the water. Several times during the bathing, speak the words of consecration.

• After the bathing, consecrate yourself with Abramelin Oil. Use your right forefinger to make the sign of the Rose Cross over your heart, while speaking the words of consecration.

• Now clear your mind in meditation for a few minutes, then put on your robe, and the solar amulet, which was described in chapter 15. [It would be acceptable to wear all four amulets described in chapter 15, if you are so inclined.] You are now ready to move to the circle area, and begin the invocation.

3) Perform the Banishing Ritual of the Serpent.

4) After the banishing, move to the west side of the altar facing the east. Then move deosil around the altar, to the south. Light the white candle there and moving deosil,

light the other three. Then return to the west side of altar, facing east.

5) Move deosil to the east side of the altar and light the incense in the censer. Then move to the easternmost yellow candle and light it. Moving deosil, light the other five candles around the circle, and then move back to the west side of the altar, facing east.

6) With the butt of the dagger, strike the altar once and state "I am (your name and grades, if any)."

7) State the oath: "Hear me and know that I am now going to invoke the spirit and power of SOL, so I may obtain the Vision of the Harmony of Things, learn of the forces of Light and Beauty, and to improve my abilities to advance spiritually. I will not leave this circle until I succeed in this operation because it is necessary for me to progress in my spiritual attainment!" Then, knock once with the butt of the dagger on the altar.

8) Walk around the altar to your left and move to the easternmost point of the circle. Make a sharp right turn and circumambulate deosil six times, making the sign of Horus or The Enterer in the east. Stop after the sixth circumambulation and return deosil to the west side of the altar, facing east.

9) Pick up the wand in your right hand and the cup in your left. Hold them overhead and knock them together six times in three batteries of two (knock 2 times, pause, knock 2 times, pause, and knock 2 times). Then begin the conjurations:

[The author here yields to the poetic genius of Aleister Crowley; for he has yet to compose a solar invocation which proves as effective as the Master Therion's "Hymn to

Apollo." This was originally published in 1906, in Volume 2 of *The Collected Works of Aleister Crowley*. Additionally, at this point, the magician should assume the God-form of Ra, as described in Appendix B, and maintain that form through Step 10.]

God of the golden face and fiery forehead!
Lord of the Lion's house of strength, exalted
In the Ram's horns! O ruler of the vaulted
  Heavenly hollow!
Send out thy rays majestic, and the torrid
Light of thy song! thy countenance most splendid
Bend to the suppliant on his face extended!
  Hear me, Apollo!

Let thy fierce fingers sweep the lyre forgotten!
Recall the ancient glory of thy chanted
Music that thrilled the hearts of men, and haunted
  Life to adore thee!
Cleanse thou our market-places begotten!
Fire in my heart and music to my paean
Lend, that my song bow, past the empyrean,
  Phoebus, before thee!

All the old worship in this land is broken;
Yet on my altar burns the ancient censer,
Frankincense, saffron, galbanum, intenser!
  Ornaments glisten.
Robes of thy colour binds me for thy token.
My voice is fuller in thine adoration.
Thine image holds its god-appointed station.
  Lycian, listen!

My prayers more eloquent than older chants
Long since grown dumb on the soft forgetful airs—
My lips are loud to herald thee: my prayers
  Keener to follow.
I do aspire, as thy long sunbeam slants

Upon my crown; I do aspire to thee
As no man yet—I am in ecstasy!
      Hear me, Apollo!

My chant wakes elemental flakes of light
Flashing along the sandal-footed floor.
All listening spirits answer and adore
      Thee, the amazing!
I follow to the eagle-baffling sight,
Limitless oceans of abounding space;
Purposed to blind myself, but know thy face,
      Phoebus, in gazing.

O hear me! hear me! hear me! for my hands,
Dews deathly bathe them; sinks the stricken song;
Eyes that were feeble have become the strong,
      See thee and glisten.
Blindness is mine; my spirit understands,
Weighs out the offering, accepts the pain,
Hearing the paean of the unprofane!
      Lycian, listen!

Gods of the fiery face, the eyes inviolate!
Lords of soundless thunders, lightnings lightless!
Hear me now, for joy that I see thee sightless,
      Fervent to follow.
Grant one boon; destroy me, let me die elate,
Blasted with light intolerant of a mortal,
That the undying in me pass thy portal!
      Hear me, Apollo.

Hear me, or if about thy courts be girded
Paler some purple softening the sunlight
Merciful, mighty, O divide the one light
      Into a million
Shattered gems, that I mingle in my worded
Measures some woven filament of passion
Caught, Phoebus, from thy star-girt crown, to fashion
      Poet's pavilion.

> Let me build for thee an abiding palace
> Rainbow-hued to affirm thy light divided,
> Yet where starry words, by thy soul guided,
>   Sing as they glisten,
> Dew-drops diamonded from the abundant chalice!
> Swoons the prayer to silence; pale the altar
> Glows at thy presence as the last words falter—
>   Lycian, listen!

10) Then, with your wand, make the Invoking Hexagram of the Sun overhead while vibrating "ARARITA." Then touch wand to the center of the hexagram and vibrate "YEHUWAU ALOAH VEDOTH." And then, the solar forces shall fill your circle and completely envelop everything in the confines with solar energy. Bask in the power and absorb all the energy that flows toward you.

11) Closing the temple:

• When the time is right, rise (if you are sitting) and extinquish the yellow candles, starting in the east and moving widdershins; and then, still moving widdershins, return to the west side of the altar and face east.

• Perform the Banishing Ritual of the Serpent.

• Hold your dagger above your head and say, "And now I say unto thee, depart in peace unto thine habitations and abodes—and may the blessings of the highest be upon thee in the name of (vibrate) ARARITA—YEHUWAU ALOAH VEDOTH, and let there be peace between thee and me; and be thou very ready to come, whensoever thou art invoked and called, either by a word, or by a will or by this mighty conjuration of Magick Art."

• Then with the butt of the dagger, strike the top of the altar ten times. First 3 times, pause, then 4 times, pause, then 3 times, and say, "I now declare this temple duly closed." Then strike the altar once.

CHAPTER 19

THE EUCHARIST RITUAL

The consumation of the eucharist is one of the most basic, yet important practices of high magick. For some odd reason, the subject is neglected in virtually every modern magickal textbook, save one. That exception is none other than *Magick in Theory and Practice*, in which the first section of chapter 20 is devoted to the eucharist.

Most people are familiar with the Christian eucharist, in which the masses consume a small wafer, which is symbolic of the flesh of Christ. In conjunction with the wafer, a small glass of wine should be consumed, to represent the blood of Christ. A study of the chapter of Crowley's book mentioned previously would reveal this Christian eucharist as that of two elements. The most powerful eucharist for the ritual magician to consume, however, is that of a single element.

The identity of this sacrament is veiled in mystery, and to my knowledge, has never been specifically revealed in any published text. Aleister Crowley does provide a rather substantial clue in his textbook, as follows: "It is one substance, and not two, not living and not dead, neither liquid nor solid, neither hot nor cold, neither male nor female."[1] This riddle has been profusely misinterpreted, resulting in a variety of unsuitable sacraments; but all have been profane, compared to the true solution, "the Medicine of Metals, the Stone of the Wise, the Potable Gold, the Elixir of Life that is consumed therein."[2] This secret sacrament is simply the yolk of an egg.

---

[1]*Magick in Theory and Practice* (New York: Castle Books, n.d.), p. 179.
[2]*Magick in Theory and Practice* (New York: Castle Books, n.d.), p. 180.

As incomprehensible as this may sound to many students, the following formulae strongly supports this conclusion. The egg yolk represents the sun of the universe existing within the shell. The sun represents the "son," or crucified God. Iacchus is the "babe in the egg," which represents the path to the divine. Also, the yolk is the heart and the spirit of the egg, as so in human beings. Qabalistically, the shell is the "Qliphoth" around the "fruit of the Tree of Life," the yolk. Thelemically, the yolk is Nuit to the shell of Hadit, and a perfect representation of God within human. The whiteness of the shell symbolizes purity. The gold of the yolk is the power and strength of Tiphereth. The yolk is also an infant or embryo, and may be considered a male child, or the "babe in the egg." The egg yolk is the eucharist of a single element, and the following ritual has been composed by the author (with the assistance of Mr. Crowley) to be performed for the sole purpose of consuming the most sacred sacrament of Life. This should be performed on a daily basis by the practicing magician.

A Ritual For the Eucharist of One Element

1) The circle should be prepared as in Step 1-A of "A Lunar Invocation." The altar should be prepared in advance, with setup as follows:

• A single white candle should be placed in the east, north, west, and south.

• Each magickal weapon should be on top the altar in its respective direction.

• The censer in the east, using frankincense incense.

• A vial of Abramelin Oil in the south.

• A bowl of hyssop-treated, natural water in the west.

- A dish of natural salt in the north.

- In the center of the altar should be a wineglass, and in it should sit a whole, fresh egg, wrapped in white silk cloth. [It is best to purchase fresh eggs from a vegetable market, rather than refrigerated supermarket eggs.] Also, a small empty glass bowl should be next to the wineglass.

2) The magician should first take the ritual bath in hyssop-treated water, speaking the words of purification at some time while bathing.

3) After bathing, and before entering the circle area, the magician should make the mark of the Rose Cross over his or her heart in Abramelin Oil, while speaking the words of consecration. Then don the robe and all four amulets, and enter the circle area, moving to the west side of the altar, facing east.

4) Perform the Banishing Ritual of the Serpent. Then light the four white candles on the altar, and the incense.

5) Clap your hands together in three batteries of two. [Clap 2 times, pause, clap 2 times, pause, clap 2 times.]

6) Lift the egg up in your left hand and unwrap it.

7) Put your right forefinger into the dish of water in the west, turn to face the west, hold the egg up and dab the water onto the shell while saying "Asperges me, EHIEH (vibrate), Hyssoppo et mundabor. Lavabis me et super nivem dealbabor."

8) Move deosil to the east side of the altar, holding the egg in your left hand. Hold the egg over the censer and in the smoke, then turn to face the east, hold the egg before you and say, "Of pure will, unassuaged of purpose, in every way perfect." Then vibrate YEHUWAU.

9) Move deosil to the south side of the altar, still holding the egg in your left hand. Dab oil on your right forefinger and, facing the south, make the sign of the Rose Cross on the egg's shell, and say, "Accendat in nobis ADONAI (vibrate) ignem sui amoris et flammam aeternae caritatis."

10) Move deosil to the north side of the altar, with the egg in your left hand. Put your right forefinger into the dish of salt, face the north and dab a bit of salt on the eggshell, and say, "I am uplifted in thine heart, and the kisses of the stars rain hard upon my body." Then vibrate AGLA.

11) Move deosil to the east again, and transfer the egg to your right hand.

12) Face the east, and with the egg, make the Invoking Pentagram of the Equilibrium of Actives while vibrating EHIEH. Over top of that pentagram, make the Invoking Pentagram of Air while vibrating YEHUWAU. [One should assume the God-form of Shu during this step. See Appendix B.] Hold the egg in the center of the pentagrams for several seconds. You should feel a rush of warm, moist air from the east, and see a yellowish aura around the egg.

13) Move deosil to the south, and with the egg in your right hand, face the south and, with the egg, make the Invoking Pentagram of the Equilibrium of Actives while vibrating EHIEH. Over the top of that pentagram, make the Invoking Pentagram of Fire while vibrating ELOHIM. [Assume the God-form of Thoum-aesh-neith during this step. See Appendix B.] Hold the egg in the center of the pentagrams for several seconds. You should feel a rush of hot, dry, wind from the south, and see a reddish aura around the egg.

14) Move deosil to the west, and with the egg in your right hand, face the west and, with the egg, make the Invoking Pentagram of the Equilibrium of Passives while vibrating

AGLA. Over the top of that pentagram, make the Invoking Pentagram of Water while vibrating EL. [Assume the God-form of Auramoth during this step. See Appendix B.] Hold the egg in the center of the pentagrams for several seconds. You should feel a rush of cool, wet, wind from the west, and see a bluish aura around the egg.

15) Move deosil to the north, and with the egg in your right hand, face the north and, with the egg, make the Invoking Pentagram of the Equilibrium of Passives while vibrating AGLA. Over the top of that pentagram, make the Invoking Pentagram of Earth while vibrating ADONAI. [Assume the God-form of Apophis during this step. See Appendix B.) Hold the egg in the center of the pentagrams for several seconds. The cold, dry feeling of earth would barely be detectable, although the aura should be an earthy green-brown.

16) Still facing the north, hold the egg upward and say, "Of earth." Move deosil to the east, hold the egg high and say, "Of air." Move deosil to the south, hold the egg high and say, "Of fire." Move deosil to the west, hold the egg high and say "And of water." [The movement should be continuous.]

17) Still on the west side of the altar, turn to face the east. Carefully crack the egg open, and drain the white of the egg into the empty glass bowl [not the ritual goblet]. Then set the yolk of the egg into the wineglass, still in the center of the altar [again, not the ritual goblet]. Discard the shells into the dish of salt. Then with the wineglass, make the invoking pentagram of the sun while vibrating ARARITA. Hold the wineglass in the center of the hexagram and vibrate YEHUWAU ALOAH VEDOTH.

18) Holding the yolk in the wineglass with both hands before you, perform "The Middle Pillar Ritual" outlined in

chapter 4. After all the chakras are energized, your whole body should be aglow, as should be the wineglass before you. When the time seems right, consume the eucharist, and return the wineglass to the center of the altar. This is usually an excellent moment to meditate briefly.

19) Perform the Banishing Ritual of the Serpent.

20) When the time seems right, perform the release as follows: "I now release any spirit that may have been imprisoned by this ritual. Depart in peace to your abodes and habitations, and go with the blessings of ARARITA— YEHUWAU ALOAH VEDOTH."

21) With the dagger, strike the top of the altar in two batteries of three, divided by one battery of four. [Strike 3 times, pause, 4 times, pause, 3 times.] Then say, "This temple is duly closed," and strike once.

CHAPTER 20

INITIATION

An initiation is a ritual composed of several organized magicians, of a certain grade, in a certain order; and one individual of a lesser grade, or without formal grade, who is the focus of the entire ritual. It should symbolize the death of the latter, and their rebirth as a new magician, an initiate.

Most of the rituals outlined in this book are directed toward the solitary practitioner.[1] However, an initiation can never be self-performed, save for one exception, and this is no simple task. The only acceptable form of self-performed initiation must be performed by the individual on the astral plane. One must create the exact conditions required for celestial influences to assist the operation. This ritual is complex, and must be performed four times over the course of one year, at the exact moments of each seasonal solstice and equinox, in order to ensure a successful initiation.

What is required for the uninitiated is that you project yourself above the terran plane, and astrally create a temple with specific layout and detail, with every required object in its appropriate place. Then, you must invoke the presence of certain deities, and in the case of this particular ritual, you will invoke Egyptian deities to perform this ritual. The details and dialogue are laid out here in outline, and these next pages must be copied into your magickal records, studied and memorized over a period of not less than three months. This temple should be constructed in

---

[1]Although many can easily be adapted to fit with a group, using one person as the primary speaker. One should never take it upon oneself to divide a ritual into speaking parts for several, unless that ritual dictates such.

your mind over and over again, before the actual performance begins.

For the first thirty days of study, simply read through
the ritual thoroughly, without attempting to memorize it.
This should be done every night of the first month, just
before going to sleep. During the second month, the ritual
should be broken down into four equal parts, and each part
studied individually for one week, again before bedtime.
The third month should be devoted to completely memorizing the ritual in its entirety.[2]

Although this ritual is based on the neophyte ritual of
the order of the Golden Dawn, it should be clear that no
legitimate magickal order would accept this form of self-
initiation as an equivalent grade of that order. Additionally, for the individual who has been initiated as a
neophyte of the Golden Dawn, or as a minerval[3] of the
Ordo Templi Orientis, the following ritual would no doubt
prove redundant. If you have lost touch, or severed ties,
with your respective order, however, you could adapt the
following format toward self-advancement, using the ritual outlines detailed in Regardie's *The Golden Dawn*, or
Francis King's *Secret Rituals of the O.T.O.*, respectively.

Although the dedicated order members will argue that
no self-performed initiation could ever possibly be effective, the first law of ritual magick should be that every act is
possible. It is merely a matter of knowing what forces to
apply, and where, when and how to apply them. By
intensely studying this ritual, you are feeding your mind
the material needed to create the circumstances necessary
for this initiation to occur on the astral plane. Then by
invoking the proper celestial influences in their proper

---

[2]All events and results should be duly recorded also, for future study and com-
parison.

[3]Minerval initiation is the first grade of the Ordo Templi Orientis (OTO) initiation
system, referred to as O = O degree. This is roughly equivalent to the neophyte
initiation of the Golden Dawn. The initiate who has undergone minerval initiation must then prepare to undertake the first degree initiation.

places and in the proper order, you are encouraging their assistance. When properly performed, this self-initiation ritual has stimulated profound experience in numerous individuals. Note: The section on the neophyte ritual of the Golden Dawn, in Volume 2 of *The Golden Dawn* by Israel Regardie, should also be studied in conjunction with the performance of the following ritual.

A Self-performed Initiation Ritual

[This ritual should be performed in a circle prepared as in Step 1-A of "A Lunar Invocation." No altar will be necessary.]

1) The uninitiated should first take the ritual bath in hyssop-treated water, speaking the words of purification at some point during the ritual bathing.

2) After bathing, and before entering the circle area, the uninitiated should make the mark of the Rose Cross over his or her heart in Abramelin Oil, while speaking the words of consecration.

3) Perform the Banishing Ritual of the Serpent.

4) Within the circle, the uninitiated should astrally rise directly upward, beyond the sky of the terran plane.

5) After rising a considerable distance, when you can no longer discern any view of the terran below you, stop.

6) The details of the temple are as follows. These should be completely memorized well in advance, and the temple should have been constructed in your own mind countless times during the three-month preparation period. (Also see figure 29 on page 204.)

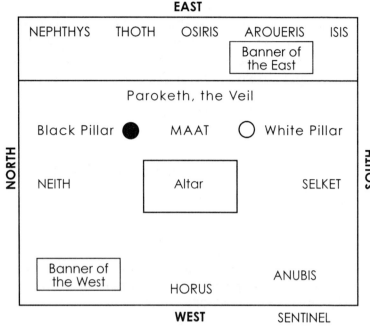

Figure 29. Temple Setup.

• The temple is square, with each flat side facing the four directions: east, west, north and south.

• It has white walls inside and outside, with a white floor. The ceiling is open to the skies.

• Within the interior stands one square altar in the center, with each flat side facing the four directions. Additionally, there are four square altars, each one centered against one of the interior walls, except for the eastern altar.

• To the east of the center altar stands two pillars. To the northeast, a black pillar; and to the southeast, a white pillar. The eastern altar should be placed between the black and white pillars.

• There should be a doorway, or portal, on the west wall toward the southwest corner. This is oval-shaped, and draped in white silk.

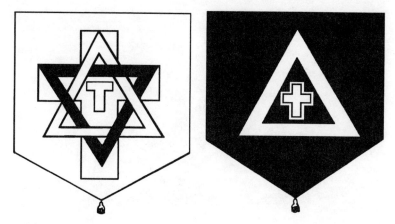

Figure 30. The Banners of the East and West. The Banner of the East features a white background and a center cross of white, with the upright triangle in red, the inverted triangle in blue, and the large cross in yellow. The Banner of the West features a black background, a large white triangle, and in the center, a red cross outlined in yellow.

• There should be "The Banner of the West" (see figure 30 above) by the western wall, directly between the western altar and the northwest corner.

• To the east is a white silk curtain in place where the eastern wall would center the room, although the solid wall should be four feet beyond the curtain. The curtain is known as "Paroketh, the Veil." Between the curtain and the wall should be "The Banner of the East" (figure 31) situated between the center of the eastern wall and the southeast corner. [Of course, the curtain will conceal "The Banner of the East," but you will know it is there.]

• On top of the center altar, will be a white cross facing the east, and a red triangle facing west. Additionally, there will be a freshly cut rose in the east, a red lamp in the south, a goblet of wine in the west, and a paten of bread and salt in the north. (See figure 31, page 206.)

Figure 31. Altar Setup.

7) After the temple is completed, the uninitiated should be dressed in a robe of flowing black silk, and red shoes.

8) Then the Lesser Banishing Ritual of the Pentagram should be performed, followed by the Lesser Banishing Ritual of the Hexagram, to remove any unwanted influences.

9) The next step is to invoke Osiris, Aroueris, Thoth, Isis, and Nephthys to preside over the operation from between the eastern curtain and the eastern wall, behind the Veil of Paroketh. (While performing these invocations, you should assume the corresponding God-form, as outlined in Appendix B.) Move to the center of the curtain in the east, and use the invoking hexagrams as follows, and in the following order. [The uninitiated should never travel beyond the veil

of Paroketh, and all symbols drawn should be with the finger only. The uninitiated must at all times, remain unarmed.]

• Invoke Osiris directly in the center of the eastern wall by using your finger to draw the Invoking Hexagram of Jupiter while vibrating ARARITA, and then touching the center of the hexagram, while vibrating OSIRIS. Then say forcibly, "I invoke thee, OSIRIS! Your presence is required in the temple of initiation."

• Move directly between the center and southeast corner of the eastern wall, and there invoke Aroueris with the Invoking Hexagram of Mars while vibrating ARARITA, and then touching the center of the hexagram, while vibrating AROUERIS. Then say forcibly, "I invoke thee, AROUERIS! Your presence is required in the temple of initiation."

• Then move to directly between the center and northeast corner of the eastern wall, and invoke Thoth with the Invoking Hexagram of Mercury, in the same fashion.

• Move to just north of the southeast corner of the eastern wall, and invoke Isis with the Invoking Hexagram of Venus, in the same fashion.

• Move to just south of the northeast corner of the eastern wall, and invoke Nephthys with the Invoking Hexagram of Saturn, in the same fashion.

10) The next step is to invoke Maat, Selket, Horus, and Neith in the four elemental directions within the main room of the temple. Use the invoking pentagrams as listed, and in the following order:

• Before the altar in the east, invoke Maat with the Invoking Pentagram of Air, while vibrating YEHUWAU. Touch your finger to the center of the pentagram, and vibrate MAAT. Then say, "I invoke thee, MAAT! Your presence is required in the temple of initiation." [One should assume the God-form of the Goddess Thmaa-est while invoking Maat.]

• Then move to stand before the altar in the north, and invoke Selket with the Invoking Pentagram of Fire, while vibrating ELOHIM. Touch the center of the pentagram, and vibrate SELKET. [Assume the God-form of Thaum-aesh-nieth.]

• Then move to stand before the altar in the west, and invoke Horus with the Invoking Pentagram of Water, while vibrating EL. Touch the center of the pentagram, and vibrate HORUS. [Assume the God-form of Harpocrates.]

• Then move to stand before the altar in the north, and invoke Neith with the Invoking Pentagram of Earth, while vibrating ADONAI. Touch the center of the pentagram, and vibrate NEITH. [Assume the God-form of Auramoth.]

11) The next step is to invoke Anubis in the southwest corner of the temple. Use the invoking hexagram of Earth, while vibrating ARARITA, and then touching the center of the hexagram, while vibrating ANUBIS. [Assume the God-form of Anubis.] Then say, "I invoke thee, ANUBIS! Your presence is required in the temple of initiation."

12) Then the initiate should exit through the oval portal on the west wall, and outside the temple, invoke the Sentinel by using the invoking hexagram of earth, in the same manner as in the last step. [IMPORTANT! When assuming the God-form of Anubis to invoke the Sentinel, one should envision the nemyss, all clothing and ornaments to be black and white.]

13) Then wait just outside the temple. The following dialogue should occur within the temple:

[The uninitiated will not be able to see the goings on within the temple, but should be able to hear the words spoken. These words should be fully memorized, and the uninitiated should follow along mentally, hearing the words that should be said and visualizing the activity that is occuring within the temple. In a sense, you are creating this initiation with your mind.]

[First, one knock.]

Anubis: Hekas, Hekas, Este Bebeloi.

[One knock.]

Osiris: Brothers and sisters, asssist me to open the temple of initiation. Brother Anubis, see that the hall is properly guarded.

[One knock, pause, one knock.]

Anubis: Very honored Osiris, the hall is properly guarded.

Osiris: Honored Horus, guard the hither side of the portal, and assure yourself that all present have beheld the Morning Star.

Horus: Brothers and sisters, give the signs of the neophyte. (pause) Very honored Osiris, all present have been so honored.

Osiris: Let the number of officers of the grade, and the nature of their offices be proclaimed once again, that the powers whose images they are be re-awakened in the spheres of those present, and in the sphere of the order, for it is by names and images that all powers are awakened and re-awakened (pause). Honored Horus, how many chief officers are there in this grade?

Horus: Their are three chief officers: the Hierophant, Hierus, and Hegemon.

Osiris: Is there any peculiarity in these names?

Horus: They all commence with the letter "H."

Osiris: Of what is this letter a symbol?

Horus: Of life, because the letter "H" is our mode of representing the ancient Greek aspirate or breathing, and breath is the evidence of life.

Osiris: How many lesser officers are there?

Horus: Their are three, besides the Sentinel: Anubis, Neith, and Selket. The sentinel is without the portal of the hall, and has a sword in his hand to keep out intruders. It is his duty to prepare the candidate.

Osiris: Sister Selket, your stations and duties?

Selket: My station is the south, to symbolize heat and dryness, and my duty is to see that the lamp and fires of the temple are ready at the opening, to watch over the censer and incense, and to consecrate the hall and the brothers and sisters and the candidate with fire.

Osiris: Sister Neith, your station and duties?

Neith: My station is in the north, to symbolize cold and moisture. My duties are to see that the robes and collars and insignia of the officers are ready at the opening and to watch over the cup of lustral water. I purify the hall, the brothers and sisters, and the candidate with water.

Osiris: Brother Anubis, your station and duties?

Anubis: My place is within the portal. My duties are to see that the furniture of the hall is properly arranged at the opening, to guard the inner side of the portal, to admit the brothers and sisters, and to watch over the reception of the candidate; to lead all mystic circumambulations carrying the lamp of my office, and to make all reports and announcements. My lamp is the symbol of the hidden knowledge, and my wand is the symbol of its directing power.

Osiris: Honored Maat, your station and duties?

Maat: My station is between the two pillars of Hermes and Solomon, and my face is toward the cubical altar of the universe. My duty is to watch over the gateway of the hidden knowledge, for I am the reconciler between light and darkness. I watch over the preparation of the candidate, and assist in his or her reception, and I lead the candidate in the path that conducts from darkness to light. The white color of my robe is the color of purity, my ensign of office is a miter-headed scepter to symbolize religion, which guides and regulates life, and my office symbolizes those higher aspirations of the soul which should guide its action.

Osiris: Honored Horus, your station and duties?

Horus: My station is on the throne of the west, and is a symbol of increase of darkness and decrease of light, and I am the master of darkness. I keep the gateway of the west, and watch over the reception of the candidate, and over the lesser officers in the doing of their work. My black robe is an image of the darkness that was upon the face of the waters. I carry the sword of judgment and the banner of the evening twilight, which is the "Banner of the West," and I am called Fortitude by the unhappy.

Osiris: My station is on the throne of the east in the place where the Sun rises, and I am the master of the hall, governing it according to the laws of the order, as

HE, whose image I am, is the master of all who work for the hidden knowledge. My robe is red because of uncreated fire and created fire, and I hold the banner of the morning light, which is the "Banner of the East." I am called power and mercy and light and abundance, and I am the expounder of the mysteries. (Pause.) Sister Neith and sister Selket, I command you to purify and consecrate the hall with water and with fire.

[The actions of purification and consecration will be observed later on in the ritual, but are not seen at this point.]

[Pause.]

Neith: I purify with water.

[Pause.]

Selket: I consecrate with fire.

[Pause.]

Osiris: Let the mystic circumambulation take place in the pathway of light.

[One minute pause.]

Osiris: The mystic circumambulation symbolical of the rise of LIGHT is accomplished. Let us adore the Lord of the universe and space. [Pause.] Holy art thou, Lord of the universe! [Pause.] Holy art thou, whom nature hath not formed! [Pause.] Holy art thou, the vast and mighty one! [Pause.] Lord of the light and of the darkness! [Pause.] Brother Anubis, in the name of the Lord of the universe, I command you to declare that I have opened the hall of the neophytes.

Anubis: In the name of the Lord of the universe, who works in silence and whom naught but silence can express, I declare that the Sun has arisen and the shadows flee away.

[Knock, pause, knock, pause, knock, pause, knock.]

Osiris: KHABS.

[Knock.]

Horus: AM.

[Knock.]

Maat: PEKHT.

[Knock.]

Horus: KONX.

[Knock.]

Maat: OM.

[Knock.]

Osiris: PAX.

[Knock.]

Maat: LIGHT.

[Knock.]

Osiris: IN.

[Knock.]

Horus: EXTENSION.

[Pause.]

Osiris: Brothers and sisters, I have recieved a dispensation from the greatly honored chiefs of the second order, to admit (candidate's name) to the O = O degree of neophyte. Honored Maat, bid the candidate prepare for the ceremony of admission, and superintend the candidate's preparation.

14) The uninitiated should have been waiting just outside the portal. At this point, Maat exits through the portal to where the candidate waits. The sentinel should then blindfold the candidate, and with hands at sides, wrap a rope three times around his or her waist. [If the candidate cannot discern this happening, he or she should close the eyes, leaving arms at sides, and walk toward the portal, as if aware of what should be happening.] Maat then should knock once on the outer door of the portal. Anubis should return the knock once from within the portal, and the following dialogue should then occur within the temple:

Anubis: The candidate seeks for entrance.

Osiris: I give permission to admit (candidate's name), who now loses his or her name, and will henceforth be known among us as (the candidate's magical motto). Let Neith and Selket assist in the reception.

15) At this point, Maat should go through the portal, followed by the candidate, who is followed by the sentinel. They should all move in the hall, and Maat should move aside. The blindfolded candidate faces Anubis, with Neith and Selket standing behind him or her, in a triangular formation. The sentinel remains at the portal, behind the candidate. The following dialogue should then occur:

Maat: Inheritor of a dying world, arise and enter the darkness.

Neith: The mother of darkness hath blinded him/her with Her hair.

Selket: The Father of darkness hath hidden him/her under His wings.

Osiris: His/her limbs are still weary from the wars which were in Heaven.

Anubis: Unpurified and unconsecrated, thou canst not enter our sacred hall.

16) Then Neith comes forward, dips her thumb in the lustral water, and makes a cross on the candidate's brow with it. She then sprinkles him or her three times, saying, "I purify thee with water."

17) Then Selket comes forward, and with the censer, makes a cross over the candidate, waving it three times, saying, "I consecrate thee with fire."

18) Then the following dialogue should occur:

Osiris: Conduct the candidate to the foot of the altar. Inheritor of a dying world, why seekest thou to enter our sacred hall? Why seekest thou admission to our order?

[The candidate should not answer Osiris. Maat will speak for the candidate at this point.]

Maat: My soul wanders in darkness, and seeks the light of the hidden knowledge, and I believe that in this order, knowledge of that light may be obtained.

Osiris: We hold your signed pledge to keep secret everything that relates to this order. I now ask you: are you willing to take a solemn obligation in the presence of this assembly, to keep the secrets and mysteries of our order inviolate?

Candidate: I AM! [Speak out loud, and forcibly!]

Osiris: There is nothing contrary to your civil, moral or religious duties in this obligation. Although the magickal virtues can indeed awaken into momentary life in wicked and foolish hearts, they cannot reign in any heart that has not the natural virtues to be their throne. He who is the fountain of the spirit of man and

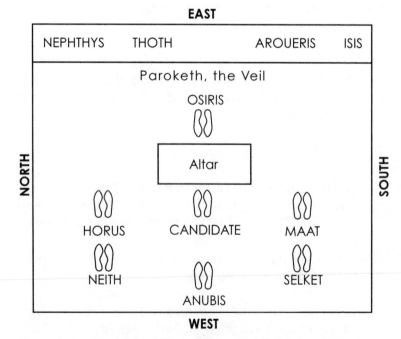

Figure 32. Position of the Officers in Step 19 of the Initiation Ritual.

of things, came not to break, but to fulfill the law. Are you ready to take this oath?

Candidate: I AM READY!

Osiris: Then kneel on both your knees.

19) Now Maat leads the still-blindfolded candidate to the west side of the altar, facing east. She then assists him or her to a kneeling position, and then stands three feet to the candidate's right. All are facing the east. Horus stands three feet to the candidate's left, Neith stands three feet directly behind Horus, Selket stands three feet directly behind Maat, and Anubis stands six feet directly behind the candidate. Osiris moves to the east side of the altar, facing west. [See figure 32.] Then the following dialogue should occur:

Osiris: Give me your right hand, which I place upon this Holy symbol. Place your left hand in mine, bow your head, repeat your full name by which you are known on earth, and say after me: I, (candidate's name), in the presence of the LORD of the universe, who works in silence and whom naught but silencecan express, and in this hall of the neophytes, regularly assembled under warrant from the greatly honored chiefs of the second order, do, of my own free will, hereby and hereon, most solemnly promise to keep secret this order, from every person in the world who has not been initiated into it; I undertake to maintain a kindly and benevolent relation with all brothers and sisters of this order. I solemnly promise not to suffer myself to be placed in such a state of passivity, that any person or power may cause me to lose control of my words or actions. I solemnly promise to persevere with courage and determination in the labors of the Divine science, even as I shall persevere with courage and determination through this ceremony, which is their image—and I will not debase my mystical knowledge in the labor of evil magic at any time tried or under any temptation.

I swear upon this Holy symbol to observe all these things without evasion, equivocation, or mental reservation, under the penalty of being expelled from this order for my perjury and my offence.

Furthermore, if I break this, my magickal obligation, I submit myself, by my own consent, to a stream of power, set in motion by the divine guardians of this order, who live in the light of their perfect justice, and before whom my soul now stands. They journey as upon the winds— They strike where no man strikes— They slay where no man slays—and, as I do bow my neck under the sword of Horus, so do I commit myself unto their hands for vengeance or reward.

So help me, my mighty and secret soul, and the Father of my soul, who works in silence and whom naught but silence can express.

20) Then Osiris says, "Rise neophyte, of the O = O grade of the order."

21) Osiris returns to his throne, behind the veil of Paroketh. Horus returns to his place in the west, and Maat assists the candidate to his or her feet. The following dialogue then occurs:

> *Osiris*: Honored Maat, you will now place the neophyte in the northern part of the hall—the place of forgetfulness, dumbness, and necessity, and of the greatest symbolical darkness.

22) Maat assists the candidate to walk to the northern part of the temple, facing the east. Anubis walks to the northeast, carrying the lamp and wand. Neith and Selket follow behind Anubis. The following dialogue then occurs:

Osiris: The voice of the undying and secret soul said unto me, "Let the candidate enter the path of darkness and, peradventure, there shall I find the light. I am the only being in an abyss of darkness; from an abyss of darkness came I forth ere my birth, from the silence of a primal sleep. And the voice of ages answered to my soul—'I am He who formulates in darkness—the light that shineth in darkness, yet darkness comprehendeth it not.' " Let the mystic circumambulation take place in the path of knowledge, that leadeth unto light, with the lamp of hidden knowledge to guide us.

23) The circumambulations begin. [Deosil.] Anubis leads, followed by Maat with the candidate, and Neith and Selket behind. Osiris knocks once as the candidate passes the east side of the altar. Horus knocks once as the candidate passes the west side of the altar. Osiris knocks once again as the candidate passes, but Anubis stops in the south, and bars the way with his wand, and says, "Unpurified and unconsecrated, thou canst not enter the path of the west!"

24) Neith comes forward, dips her thumb in water, and makes a cross on the candidate's brow. She then sprinkles the candidate three times, saying, "I purify thee with water."

25) Selket comes forward, and with the censer, makes a cross over the candidate, waving it three times saying, "I consecrate thee with fire." Neith and Selket then step back to their places, behind the candidate. Then Maat says, "Child of Earth, twice purified and twice consecrated, thou mayest approach the gateway of the west."

26) Anubis leads the procession to the west side of the altar, before Horus. Maat then lifts the blindfold, and Horus

stands before the candidate, with sword drawn. The following dialogue occurs:

> *Horus*: Thou canst not pass by me, saith the Guardian of the west, unless thou canst tell me my name.

> *Maat*: Darkness is thy name, thou great one of the paths of the shades.

> *Horus*: Thou hast known me now, so pass thou on. Fear is failure so be thou without fear. For he who trembles at the flame, and at the flood, and at the shadows of the air, hath no part in God.

27) Maat redoes the blindfold, and Anubis leads the procession onward. Horus knocks once as the candidate passes. Then Anubis stops in the north, raises his wand, and says, "Unpurified and unconsecrated, thou canst not enter the path of the east!"

28) Neith then crosses and sprinkles with water, as in Step 16.

29) Selket then crosses and waves censer, as in Step 17.

30) Then Maat says, "Child of Earth, thrice purified and thrice consecrated, thou mayest approach the gateway of the east!"

31) Then Anubis leads the procession to the east side of the altar, before Osiris. Maat then lifts the blindfold, and Osiris stands before the candidate, with scepter drawn. The following dialogue occurs:

> *Osiris*: Thou canst not pass by me, saith the guardian of the east, unless thou canst tell me my name.

> *Maat*: Light dawning in darkness is thy name, the light of a golden day.

Osiris: Unbalanced power is the ebbing away of life.

Unbalanced mercy is weakness and the fading out of the will.

Unbalanced severity is cruelty and the barrenness of mind.

Thou hast known me now, so pass thou on to the cubical altar of the universe.

32) Maat redoes the blindfold, and Anubis leads the procession onwards deosil, to the altar. The candidate is assisted to the west side of the altar, facing east. The procession returns to the same positions as in Step 19. Osiris advances between the pillars, carrying the scepter in his right hand, and the Banner of the East in his left hand. He moves to the east side of the altar, facing the candidate. The following dialogue occurs:

Osiris: I come in the power of the light. I come in the light of the wisdom. I come in the mercy of the light. The light hath healing in its wings.

33) The officers now form a hexagram around the altar, as in figure 32 (page 216). Horus holds his sword in his right hand and the Banner of the West in his left. All officers, except Osiris, kneel down, and the candidate is assisted to his or her knees. Osiris raises his hands, holding the scepter and banner, and the following dialogue occurs:

Osiris: Lord of the universe—the vast and the mighty one! Ruler of the light and of the darkness!

We adore thee and we invoke thee!

Look with favor on this neophyte who now kneeleth before thee.

And grant thine aid unto the higher aspirations of his or her soul,

So that this candidate may prove a true and faithful brother/sister neophyte among us.

To the glory of thine ineffable name. Amen!

34) All rise, the candidate is assisted to rise, and then brought close to the altar. Osiris, Horus, and Maat raise their wands and swords to touch each other above the head of the candidate. The following dialogue occurs:

Maat: Inheritor of a dying world, we call thee to the living beauty.

Horus: Wanderer in the wild darkness, we call thee to the gentle light. [At the word "darkness," Anubis removes the blindfold.]

Osiris: Long hast thou dwelt in darkness—Quit the night and seek the day.

Maat, Horus and Osiris together: We recieve thee into our order.

Osiris: KHABS.

Horus: AM.

Maat: PEKHT.

Horus: KONX.

Maat: OM.

Osiris: PAX.

Maat: LIGHT.

Osiris: IN.

Horus: EXTENSION.

35) The officers then take down their scepters and swords. Anubis moves to northeast of the altar, and raises the lamp.

Osiris then directs the candidate's attention to the lamp by pointing at it, and then says, "In all thy wandering in darkness, the lamp of the kerux went before thee, though it was not seen by thine eyes. It is the symbol of the light of the hidden knowledge."

36) The officers then return to their places, and Osiris to his throne behind the veil of Paroketh. Maat and the candidate remain on the west side of the altar. Osiris then says, "Let the neophyte be led to the east of the altar."

37) Maat guides the candidate to the east side of the altar, and then moves to the outside of the white pillar. Osiris says, "Honored Horus, give the neophyte the secret signs, tokens and words of the O = O grade. Place the candidate between the mystical pillars, and superintend this fourth and final consecration.

38) Horus then passes by the north, to the black pillar. He comes around to the east, and Maat advances to meet him, and takes his sword and banner. Horus steps between the pillars, and faces the candidate. The following dialogue occurs:

> *Horus*: Brother/Sister (magical motto), I shall now instruct you in the secret step, sign, grip and word of this grade. First, advance your left foot a short space, as if entering a portal. This is the step. The signs are two. The first, or saluting, sign is given thus: Lean forward and stretch both arms out thus. [The neophyte should make the sign of Horus, the Enterer, as described in chapter 12, and in Table 3, page 142]. It alludes to your condition in a state of darkness, groping for light.
>
> The second sign is the sign of Silence, and given by placing the left forefinger on your lip thus. [The neophyte should make the sign of Harpocrates, or Silence, as described in chapter 8, and figure 17, page 74]. It is

the position shown in many ancient statues of Harpocrates, and it alludes to the strict silence you have sworn to maintain concerning everything connected with this order. The first sign is always answered by the second.

The grip or token is given thus: advance your left foot touching mine, toe and heel, extend your right hand to grasp mine, fail, try again, and then succeed in touching the fingers only. It alludes to the seeking guidance in darkness. The grand word is Har-Par-Krat, and it is whispered in this position mouth to ear, in syllables. [The neophyte should exchange the word with Horus.] It is the Egyptian name for the God of silence, and should always remind you of the strict silence you have sworn to maintain.

I now place you between the two pillars of Hermes and Solomon, in the symbolical gateway of occult wisdom.

39) Horus leads the neophyte forward, and takes back the sword and banner from Maat. He moves to the northeast side of the black pillar, and says, "Let the final consecration take place."

40) Neith and Selket come forward. Neith moves first to face Osiris, and makes a cross in the air with her cup. She sprinkles a few drops of water three times toward the east, and repeats the purification in the south, west, and north. She then returns to the east, holds the cup on high, and says, "I purify with water."

41) Selket follows Neith when she goes to the east, and when she moves to the south, Selket faces east, raises her censer and swings it three times to the east, and then repeats the consecration in the south, west, and north. She then moves to the east, raises the censer and says, "I consecrate with fire."

42) As Neith returns to the east, she purifies the neophyte as was done in Step 16.

43) As Selket returns to the east, she consecrates the neophyte, as was done in Step 17.

44) Neith and Selket then return to their places. Then Osiris says, "Honored Maat, I command you to remove the rope, last remaining symbol of the path of darkness, and to invest our brother (sister) with the badge of this degree."

45) Maat then moves forward, and hands her scepter and ritual to Horus. She then removes the rope, and puts a black sash over the neophyte's left shoulder, and says, "By command of the very honored Osiris, I invest you with the badge of this degree. It symbolizes light dawning in darkness." She takes back her scepter, and returns to the white pillar.

46) Osiris then says, "Let the mystical circumambulation take place in the pathway of light."

47) Anubis then moves to the northeast; Maat takes the candidate behind the black pillar, and stands behind Anubis. Horus follows, and Neith and Selket follow Horus. Anubis then leads the procession, all saluting Osiris, who stands holding the scepter and the Banner of the East. Horus drops out after reaching his place, and Maat returns to between the pillars, after passing Osiris twice. The neophyte continues to follow Anubis, who along with Neith and Selket, passes Osiris three times. After the third passing, Osiris says, "Take your place northwest of Neith."

48) Anubis continues, followed by Neith, who drops out as they pass the north, and returns to her place. Maat sits down between the pillars, and Anubis replaces the rose, lamp, cup and paten of bread to their proper places on the altar [These

were removed before the candidate's reception.] and all are seated. Then the following dialogue occurs:

> *Osiris*: The threefold cord bound about your waist was an image of the threefold bondage of mortality, which, among the initiated, is called earthly or material inclination, that has bound into a narrow place, the once far-wandering soul; and the hoodwink was an image of the darkness, of ignorance, of mortality, that has blinded mankind to the happiness and beauty their eyes once looked upon.
>
> The double cubical altar in the center of the hall is an emblem of visible nature or the material universe, concealing within herself the mysteries of all dimensions, while revealing her surface to the exterior senses. It is a double cube because, as it is written on The Emerald Tablet, "The things that are below are a reflection of the things that are above." The world of men and women created to unhappiness is a reflection of the world of the Divine beings created to happiness. It is described in the *Sepher Yetzirah* or *Book of Formation*, as an abyss of height, and as an abyss of depth, an abyss of the east, and an abyss of the west, an abyss of the north, and an abyss of the south. The altar is black because, unlike Divine beings who unfold in the element of light, the fires of created beings arise from darkness and obscurity.
>
> On the altar is a white triangle to be the image of that immortal light, that triune light, which moves in darkness, and formed the world of darkness and out of darkness. There are two contending forces, and one always uniting them. And these three have their image in the threefold flame of our being, and in the threefold wave of the sensual world.

49) Osiris stands up, and extends his arms in the form of a cross, and says, "Glory be to thee, Father of the undying.

For thy glory flows out rejoicing, to the ends of the Earth!"
He then reseats himself. The following dialogue occurs:

Osiris: The red cross above the white triangle is an
image of Him who was unfolded in the light. At its
east, south, west and north angles are a rose, fire, cup
of wine, and bread and salt. These allude to the four
elements, air, fire, water, earth.

The mystical words, "Khabs Am Pekht," are ancient
Egyptian, and are the origin of the Greek, "Konx Om
Pax," which was uttered at the Eleusinian mysteries. A
literal translation would be, "Light rushing out in one
ray," and they signify the same form of light as that
symbolized by the staff of Anubis.

East of the double cubical altar, of created things, are the
pillars of Hermes and Solomon. On these are painted
certain hieroglyphics from the 17th and the 125th chapters of the Book of the Dead. They are the symbols of
the two powers of day and night, love and hate, work
and rest, the subtle force of the lodestone and the eternal outpouring and inpouring of the heart of God.

The lamps that burn, though with a veiled light, signify
that the pathway to hidden knowledge, unlike the
pathway of nature—which is a continual undulation,
the winding hither and thither of the Serpent—is the
straight and narrow way between them.

It was because of this that I passed between them,
when you came to the light, and it was because of this
that you were placed between them to receive the final
consecration.

Two contending forces and one which unites them
eternally. Two basal angles of the triangle and one
which forms the apex. Such is the origin of creation—
it is the triad of life.

My throne at the gate of the east is the place of the guardian of the dawning sun.

The throne of the hierus (Horus) at the gate of the west is the place of the guardian against the multitudes that sleep through the light and awaken at twilight.

The throne of the hegemon (Maat) seated between the columns is the place of balanced power, between the ultimate light and the ultimate darkness. These meanings are shown in detail and by the color of our robes.

The wand of the kerux (Anubis) is the beam of light from the hidden wisdom, and his lamp is an emblem of the ever-burning lamp of the guardian of the mysteries.

The seat of the stolistes (Neith) at the gate of the north is the place of the guardian of the cauldron and the well of water—of cold and moisture.

The seat of the dadouchos (Selket) at the gate of the south is the place of the guardian of the lake of fire and the burning bush.

Brother Anubis, I command you to declare that the neophyte has been initiated into the mysteries of the O = O grade.

50) Then Anubis advances to the northeast, faces west and raises his wand saying, "In the name of the Lord of the universe, who works in silence and whom naught but silence can express, and by command of the very honored hierophant, hear ye all, that I proclaim that (neophyte's name) who will be henceforth known as (neophyte's magical motto), has been duly admitted to the O = O grade as a neophyte of the order," and then returns to his place.

51) Then the following dialogue occurs:

Osiris: Honored Horus, I delegate to you the duty of pronouncing a short address to our brother/sister on his/her admission.

Horus: Brother/Sister (magical motto), it is my duty to deliver this exhortation to you. Remember your obligation in this order to secrecy—for strength is in silence, and the seed of wisdom is sown in silence and grows in darkness and mystery.

Remember that you hold all religions in reverence, for there is none but contains a ray from the ineffable light that you are seeking. Remember the penalty that awaits the breaker of his oath. Remember the mystery that you have recieved, and that the secret of wisdom can be discerned only from the place of balanced powers.

Study well the great arcanum of the proper equilibrium of severity and mercy, for either unbalanced is not good. Unbalanced severity is cruelty and oppression; unbalanced mercy is but weakness and would permit evil to exist unchecked, thus making itself, as it were, the accomplice of evil.

Remember that things divine are not attained by mortals who understand the body alone, for only those who are lightly armed can attain the summit.

Remember that God alone is our light and the bestower of perfect wisdom, and that no mortal power can do more than bring you to the pathway of that wisdom, which he could, if it so pleased him, put into the heart of a child. For as the whole is greater than the part, so are we but sparks from the insupportable light which is in Him.

The ends of the Earth are swept by the borders of his garment of flame—from Him all things proceed, and unto Him all things return. Therefore, we invoke

Him. Therefore even the Banner of the East falls in adoration before Him.

Osiris: Before you can pass to a higher grade, you will have to commit to memory certain rudiments of occult knowledge. You are aware of the proper texts. After four performances of this initiation ritual, on each of the equinoxes and solstices of the year, you may begin your study of these lectures. After they are committed to memory, you may begin to study the initiation ritual of the zelator, as you have studied for this ritual. [These lectures are published in *The Golden Dawn* by Israel Regardie.]

52) Then Anubis leads the neophyte to his table, and gives the neophyte one of the small dishes of solution to hold. Anubis says, "Nature is harmonious in all her workings, and that which is above is as that which is below. Also, the truths which we investigate by the physical sciences are but special examples of the natural laws of the universe. Within this pure and limpid fluid lie hidden and unperceived by mortal eyes, the elements bearing the semblance of blood, even as within the mind and brain of the initiate lie concealed the divine secrets of the hidden knowledge. Yet if the oath be forgotten, and the solemn pledge broken, then that which is secret shall be revealed, even as this pure fluid reveals the semblance of blood."

53) Anubis then adds fluid from another dish to the dish held by the neophyte, and says, "Let this remind thee ever, O, Neophyte, how easily by a careless or unthinking word, thou mayst betray that which thou hast sworn to keep secret and mayst reveal the hidden knowledge imparted to thee, and planted in thy brain and in thy mind. And let the hue of blood remind thee that if thou shalt fail in this thy oath of secrecy, thy blood may be poured out and thy body broken; for heavy is the penalty exacted by the guardians of

the hidden knowledge from those who willfully betray their trust."

54) Osiris comes to the table, and opens a book on the table. The pages contain the ritual that has just occurred, and the neophyte must sign the book with a feather quill, dipped in the bottle of red ink on the table.

55) Anubis directs the neophyte to his or her seat, and Osiris returns to his place. Then the closing begins.

56) Osiris knocks once, and Anubis walks to the northeast, faces the west, raises his lamp and wand, and says, "HEKAS! HEKAS! ESTE BEBELOI!" Anubis returns to his place.

57) Osiris says, "Brothers and sisters, assist me to close the hall of the neophytes." Then all rise.

58) Horus knocks once, then Maat knocks once, then Anubis, and then the sentinel.

59) The following dialogue occurs:

Osiris: Brother Anubis, see that the hall is properly guarded.

Anubis: The hall is properly guarded, very honored Osiris.

Osiris: Honored Horus, assure yourself that all present have beheld the Morning Star.

Horus: Brothers and sisters, give the signs. [Then the officers give their individual sign.] Very honored Osiris, all present have been so honored.

Osiris: Let the hall be purified by water and by fire.

60) Neith purifies the hall, as in Step 40.

61) Selket consecrates the hall, as in Step 41.

62) Osiris then says, "Let the mystical reverse circumambulation take place in the pathway of light."

63) Anubis moves past the south, to the southeast. Maat moves to the north, leading the neophyte past the west and south, directing him/her to follow Maat in the procession. Horus follows the neophyte, followed by Neith and Selket. The sentinel ends the procession.

64) As they pass Osiris [who is standing, holding the Banner of the East in his left hand, and the scepter in his right] all make the signs of the neophyte.

65) Horus drops out as his throne is reached. Maat passes Osiris twice, and then moves to stand between the pillars.

66) The neophyte continues to follow Anubis, who directs the neophyte to his or her seat, after passing Osiris for the third time. The other officers drop out as their places are reached.

67) Osiris then says, "The mystical reverse circumambulation is accomplished. It is the symbol of fading light. Let us adore the Lord of the Universe."

68) Then all rise [including the neophyte] and turn to face the east. Osiris, who also faces the east, makes his salute at each of the following adorations:

All present: Holy art thou, Lord of the Universe!
Holy art thou, whom nature hath not formed!
Holy art thou, the vast and mighty one!
Lord of the light and of the darkness!

69) Then all present make the sign of Silence (Harpocrates).

70) Then Osiris says, "Nothing now remains but to partake together in silence, of the mystic repast, composed of the symbols of the four elements, and to remember our pledge of secrecy." Then all are seated.

71) Osiris puts down his scepter, and returns the Banner of the East to its place. He then moves to the west side of the altar, faces east, and makes the sign of the Enterer (Horus). Then he picks up the rose from the altar, and says, "I invite you to inhale with me the perfume of this rose, as a symbol of air." He then smells the rose, and says, "To feel with me the warmth of this sacred fire." He spreads his hands over it.

72) Osiris then says "To eat with me this bread and salt as types of earth." He dips the bread into the salt, and eats it.

73) Osiris then says, "And finally to drink with me this wine, the consecrated emblem of elemental water." He makes a cross with the cup, and drinks from it. Then he sets the cup down on the altar, between the cross and triangle, and moves to the east side of the altar, facing west.

74) Then Isis moves out from behind the veil of Paroketh, and comes to the west side of the altar, faces east and makes the sign of the Enterer. Osiris responds by making the sign of Silence.

75) Osiris hands Isis the rose, which she smells and returns to him.

76) He holds the lamp, so she may feel its warmth.

77) He dips the bread in the salt, and hands it to her. She eats it.

78) He hands her the cup. She makes a cross with it, drinks and then hands it back.

79) Osiris passes by the west and south, then returning to his place. At the same moment, Isis moves to the east side of the altar.

80) Then Nephthy moves out from behind the veil of Paroketh, and comes to the west side of the altar, faces east and exchanges signs with Isis, as in Step 74. Then Steps 75 to 79 are repeated between them, and Isis returns to her place, as Nephthys moves to the east of the altar.

81) Then Thoth moves out from behind the veil of Paroketh, and comes to the west side of the altar, faces east and exchanges signs with Nephthys. Then Steps 75 to 79 are repeated between them, and Nephthys returns to her place, as Thoth moves to the east of the altar.

82) Then Aroueris moves out from behind the veil of Paroketh, and comes to the west side of the altar, faces east and exchanges signs with Thoth. Then Steps 75 to 79 are repeated between them, and Thoth returns to his place, as Aroueris moves to the east of the altar.

83) The procedure is repeated (in this order) with Horus, Maat, Neith and Selket.

84) The neophyte then takes his or her turn after Selket, and Anubis moves to take his/her place.

85) The neophyte returns to his/her place after handing the cup to Anubis. Anubis drains the cup, and then holds it inverted while saying, "It is finished!" Anubis returns the cup to the altar, and returns to his place.

86) All rise, and the following dialogue should then occur:

Osiris: [knocks once, then says] TETELESTAI!
Horus: [knocks once.]
Maat: [knocks once.]
Osiris: [knock] KHABS.
Horus: [knock] AM.
Maat: [knock] PEKHT.
Horus: [knock] KONX.
Maat: [knock] OM.
Osiris: [knock] PAX.
Maat: [knock] LIGHT.
Osiris: [knock] IN.
Horus: [knock] EXTENSION.

87) Then all make the sign of the Enterer, and then of Silence, while facing the altar. Osiris says, "May what we have partaken maintain us in our search for the QUINTES-SENCE, the stone of the philosophers. True wisdom, perfect happiness, the SUMMUM BONUM."

88) The neophyte is then led out the portal by Anubis, who immediately re-enters the temple.

89) The initiation is now complete. The neophyte should advance a short distance away from the temple, and turn to face it.

90) The neophyte should watch it, and will it to fade away, dissolve, and disappear. The neophyte should wait until no trace of it remains before departing.

91) Then the neophyte should descend to where the physical body waits within the circle, and re-enter the body.

92) Perform the Banishing Ritual of the Serpent.

93) Then hold the dagger overhead, while saying, "And now I say unto thee, depart in peace unto thine habitations

and abodes—and may the blessings of the highest be upon thee in the name of (vibrate) SHADDAI AL CHAI, and let there be peace between thee and me; and be thou very ready to come, whensoever thou art invoked and called, either by a word, or by a will or by this mighty conjuration of Magick Art." Then with the butt of the dagger, strike the top of the altar ten times. First 3 times, pause, then 4 times, pause, then 3 times, and say, "I now declare this temple duly closed." Then strike the altar once.

[Afterward, record all events in your records.]

THE HEBREW GOD-NAMES

The names to be vibrated in the rituals outlined herein are Hebrew God-names, of ancient qabalistic descent. Every name encountered and utilized by the magician should be thoroughly studied and deciphered. This study should culminate in a "formulae breakdown" of the specific name, letter by letter. These formulae should be documented in the qabalistic notebook described in chapter 10.[1] Every God-name should have a full page of interpretation devoted to it, as illustrated in chapter 5 of *Magick in Theory and Practice*, using the word VIAOV as the example.

Table 5 (see page 238) lists the Hebrew letters (which are, in fact, sigils, when properly drawn) and the numerical value designated to each one. Additionally, each letter represents a particular tarot trump, as listed in the table.

Table 6 (see page 239) illustrates the proper Hebrew spelling of the God-names of each qabalistic sephiroth, as well as a small selection of various significant names. Also outlined in Table 6 is the correct English spelling of each name, and its numerical value.

Table 7 (see page 240) is copied verbatim from a section of *777*, which gives a brief depiction of the qabalistic significance of each Hebrew letter. You should infinitely elaborate on these, on the first several pages of your own qabalistic notebook.

---

[1]This is in addition to the "Sepher Sephiroth".

Table 5. Hebrew Letters.

Hebrew Letter	Name of Letter	English Pronunciation	Numerical Value	Tarot trump Qabalistic Path
א	Aleph	A	1	0
ב	Beth	B	2	1
ג	Gimel	G	3	2
ד	Daleth	D	4	3
ה	He	H (e)	5	4
ו	Vau	V (u or oo)	6	5
ז	Zayin	Z	7	6
ח	Cheth	Ch	8	7
ט	Teth	T	9	11
י	Yod	Y (i)	10	9
ך כ	Kaph	K	20, 500	10
ל	Lamed	L	30	8
ם מ	Mem	M	40, 600	12
ן נ	Nun	N	50, 700	13
ס	Samekh	S	60	14
ע	Ayin	O (A'a)	70	15
ף פ	Peh	P	80, 800	16
ץ צ	Tzaddi	Tz	90, 900	17
ק	Qoph	Q	100	18
ר	Resh	R	200	19
ש	Shin	Sh	300	20
ת	Tau	Th	400	21

Table 6. God-Names.

Qabalistic Sephiroth	God-Names of the Sephiroth	English Spelling	Numerical Value
1. Kether	אהיה	EHIEH	21
2. Chokmah	יה	IEH	15
3. Binah	יהוה אלהים	YEHUWAU ELOHIM	112
4. Chesed	אל	EL	31
5. Geburah	אלהים נבור	ELOHIM GIBUR	297
6. Tiphereth	יהוה אלוה ודצת	YEHUWAU ELOAH VEDOTH	548
7. Netzach	יהוה צבאות	YEHUWAU TZBAOTH	525
8. Hod	אלהים צבאות	ELOHIM TZBAOTH	585
9. Yesod	שדי אל חי	SHADAI EL CHAI	363
10. Malkuth	אדני מלך	ADONAI MELECH	155

Other Significant God-Names

God-Name	English Spelling	Numerical Value
11. אנלא	AGLA (also see no. 25)	35
12. אלוה	ELOAH	42
13. אלהי	ALHI	46
14. אדני	ADONAI	65
15. אלהים	ELOHIM	86
16. בעלזבוב	BEELZEBUB	119
17. ען	ON	120
18. באבאלען	BABALON	156
19. שדי	SHADAI	314
20. נחש	NECHESH	358
21. אתה	ATOH	406
22. אבראהאדאברא	ABRAHADABRA	418
23. תריון	THERION	666
24. אראריתא	ARARITA	813
25. אחה נבור לעולם אדני	ATOH GIBUR LEOLAHM ADONAI	858

Table 7. Suggestive Correspondences from the Hebrew Alphabet.*

Hebrew	Correspondences
Aleph	The Holy Ghost—Fool—Knight-Errant. Folly's doom is ruin.
Beth	The Messenger. Prometheus. The Juggler with the Secret of the Universe.
Gimel	The Virgin. The Holy Guardian Angel is attained by Self-sacrifice and Equilibrium.
Daleth	The Wife—Alchemical Salt. The Gate of the Equilibrium of the Universe.
Hé	The Mother is the Daughter; the Daughter is the Mother.
Vau	The Sun—Redeemer. The Son is but the Son.
Zain	The Twins reconciled. The answer of the Oracles is always Death.
Cheth	The Chariot containing Life. The Secret of the Universe. Ark. Sangraal.
Teth	The Act of Power. She who rules the Secret Force of the Universe.
Yod	The Virgin Man. Secret Seed of All. Secret of the Gate of Initiation.
Kaph	The All-Father in three forms—Fire, Air and Water. In the whirlings is War.
Lamed	The Woman justified. By Equilibrium and Self-sacrifice is the Gate.
Mem	The Man drowned in the "womb" flood. The Secret is hidden between the waters that are above and the waters that are beneath.
Nun	The putrefaction in the Athanor. Initiation is guarded on both sides by Death.
Samekh	The Womb preserving Life. Self-control and Self-sacrifice govern the Wheel.
A'ain	The exalted Phallus. The Secret of generation is Death.
Pé	The Crowned and Conquering Children emerging from the Womb. The Fortress of the Most High.
Tzaddi	The Husband. Alchemical Sulfur. The Star is the Gate of the Sanctuary.
Qoph	The Womb seething is the glamour of physiological upset while the Sun sleeps. Illusionary is the Initiator of Disorder.
Resh	The Twins shining forth and playing. The fighting of Set and Osiris. In the Sun is the Secret of the Spirit.
Shin	The Stele. Nuit, Hadit, their God and Man twins, as a pantacle. Resurrection is hidden in Death.
Tau	The Slain God. Universe is the Hexagram.

*From *777 and Other Qabalistic Writings of Aleister Crowley* (York Beach, ME: Samuel Weiser, 1977), pp. 40–41.

THE EGYPTIAN GOD-FORMS

During invocation, the practitioner would find it of immense value to assume the qabalistically corresponding Egyptian God-form while drawing the appropriate symbols and vibrating the God-name. You should always envision yourself to be larger in all areas when assuming God-forms, as you are forming these bodies with your "body of desire," and in fact, cloaking your physical body with these forms. Additionally, the works of E. A. Wallis Budge, *Gods of the Egyptians*, and *The Book of the Dead*, are valuable studies for information regarding these and other Egyptian God-forms. The novice will have some difficulty seeing the variety of colors listed here, but your astral vision will improve after many hours of practice.

The God Horus (The younger, Harpocrates): Envision a face and body of translucent emerald green, with blue eyes, blue hair, and wearing a tall double crown of red and white. The collar is yellow and blue, the waistcloth is yellow and blue with a mauve girdle, and a lion's tail.

• *The sign of Silence*—as described in chapter 8; also see figure 10 (page 35).

The God Osiris: Envision a tall white Egyptian crown, flanked by feathers striped white and blue. The face is green, eyes are blue, the beard is blue and gold-tipped. Wearing a collar in bands of red, blue, yellow and black. There is a bundle strapped to the back with scarlet bands that wrap across the chest, and mummy wrappings to the feet.

• *The sign of Osiris Slain* (The Cross): as described in chapter 4; also see figure 6 (on page 32).

• *The sign of Osiris Risen* (The Pentagram): as described in chapter 4; also see figure 6 (on page 32).

The Goddess Isis: Envision a face and body of translucent gold, crowned with a throne over a vulture headdress of blue and orange, with the vulture's head being red. Wearing a blue robe, bordered with gold, and ornaments of blue and orange.

• *The sign of Isis Mourning* (The Svastika): as described in chapter 4; also see figure 6 (page 32).

The Goddess Nephthys: Envision a face and body of translucent gold, crowned with a cap over a vulture headdress of black and white, with the vulture's head being red. The collar and ornaments are black and white, wearing a black robe bordered in black and white.

The God Amoun: Envision a face and body of translucent gold, wearing an extremely tall double crown, banded in the following colors (from the bottom up): yellow at base, then indigo, violet, amber, pink, orange, and violet at top. [The large variety of colors will be difficult to envision on the first several attempts. Do the best you can, and with practice, improvement will follow.) The collar is banded in the same colors, in the same order, beginning closest to the neck and emanating outward. The eyes are blue, the beard is deep violet, the ornaments are banded in black and white, bordered in blue. The tunic is yellow, with a waist-cloth of yellow striped with blue, and a lion's tail.

The God Horus (The elder, Aroueris): Envision a double crown of red and white, with a white plume, over a nemyss of purple bands with gold edges. The face should be that of a hawk. The face and body are translucent scarlet, with green eyes and purple beard. The tunic is yellow, with a waistcloth of yellow striped with purple, and a lion's tail.

• *The sign of the Enterer*: as described in chapter 12; also see figure 10 (page 37).

The God Ra: Envision a face and body of translucent gold, wearing a gold disk between black horns as a crown, which has a red plume in back. The nemyss is gold with red edges, and the collar is banded in red and yellow. The tunic is yel-low, waistcloth of yellow striped with red, and a lion's tail.

The Goddess Hathoor: Envision a face and limbs of translu-cent gold, wearing a scarlet disk between black horns as a crown, which has two white feathers, barred in blue, rising in back. The nemyss is black, and the collar is banded in red and blue. The robe is orange, bordered with blue and red. The ornaments are blue and orange.

The Goddess Thoum-aesh-neith: Envision a red crown flanked by two feathers, barred in green and black, over a vulture headdress of red and green. The collar is red and green, and the tunic is red, and reaches to the feet.

• *The sign of the Goddess Thoum-aesh-neith*: as described in chapter 4; also see figure 5 (page 31).

Thoth: Envision the head of an Ibis, with a black beak and white throat. The nemyss is yellow, bordered with mauve. The collar is yellow with a middle band of mauve and green squares. The Tunic is mauve with yellow stripes, ornaments are red and green, and a lion's tail.

The Goddess Auramoth: Envision a blue crown with a gold plume, over a vulture headdress of orange and blue. The collar is orange and blue, and the tunic is blue, and reaches to the feet.

• *The sign of the Goddess Auramoth*: as described in chapter 4; also see figure 5 (page 31).

The God Anubis: Envision the head of a black jackal with pointed ears. The nemyss is purple-banded with white, the collar is banded in yellow and purple, and the tunic is yellow. The body is red, with a yellow and purple striped waistcloth, and a lion's tail. The ornaments are purple and gold.

The God Shu: Envision a black nemyss bound at the brow with a gold band, from which rises a tall white feather. The collar is gold, banded with scarlet, and the tunic is white, reaching to the feet. The ornaments are violet, the eyes are indigo blue, and the beard is dark purple.

• *The sign of the God Shu supporting the sky*: as described in chapter 4; also see figure 6.

The Goddess Thmaa-Est: Envision a black nemyss bound at the brow with a purple band, from which rises a tall green and red banded feather. The collar is banded red, yellow, blue and black. The tunic is emerald green, and reaches to the feet, where it is banded as is the collar. There are purple and green shoulderstraps, and a purple girdle. The armlets are emerald and red.

The God Apophis: Envision a black reptilian head, with a nemyss of olive-green and russet, and a collar of russet and citrine. The body and tail are black, wearing a white apron striped with russet, and wearing no ornaments.

- *The sign of Apophis and Typhon* (The Trident): as described in chapter 4; also see figure 6 (page 32).
- *The sign of Set fighting*: as described in chapter 4; also see figure 5 (page 31).

Liber Resh Vel Helios

BY ALEISTER CROWLEY

These adorations are to be performed daily by the ritual magician. They are from *Magick in Theory and Practice*, pp. 425–426.

0) These are the adorations to be performed by aspirants to the A∴A∴

1) Let him greet the Sun at dawn,[1] facing East, giving the sign of his grade. And let him say in a loud voice:

Hail unto Thee who art Ra in Thy rising, even unto Thee who art Ra in Thy strength, who travellest over the Heavens in Thy bark at the Uprising of the Sun.

Tahuti standeth in His splendour at the prow, and Ra-Hoor abideth at the helm.

Hail unto Thee from the Abodes of Night!

2) Also at Noon,[2] let him greet the Sun, facing South, giving the sign of his grade. And let him say in a loud voice:

Hail unto Thee who art Ahathoor in Thy triumphing, even unto Thee who art Ahathoor in Thy beauty, who travellest over the heavens in Thy bark at the Mid-course of the Sun.

---

[1] During the morning adoration, one should assume the God-form of Shu, and make the sign of "Shu supporting the sky."

[2] During the afternoon adoration, one should assume the God-form of Thoum-aesh-neith, and make the sign of "the Goddess Thoum-aesh-neith."

Tahuti standeth in His splendour at the prow, and Ra-Hoor abideth at the helm.

Hail unto Thee from the Abodes of Morning!

3) Also, at Sunset,[3] let him greet the Sun, facing West, giving the sign of his grade. And let him say in a loud voice:

Hail unto Thee who art Tum in Thy setting, even unto Thee who art Tum in Thy joy, who travellest over the heavens in Thy bark at the Down-going of the Sun.

Tahuti standeth in His splendour at the prow, and Ra-Hoor abideth at the helm.

Hail unto Thee from the Abodes of Day!

4) Lastly, at Midnight,[4] let him greet the Sun, facing North, giving the sign of his grade, and let him say in a loud voice:

Hail unto Thee who art Khephra in Thy hiding, even unto Thee who art Khephra in Thy silence, who travellest over the heavens in Thy bark at the Midnight hour of the Sun.

Tahuti standeth in His splendour at the prow, and Ra-Hoor abideth at the helm.

Hail unto Thee from the Abodes of Evening!

5) And after each of these invocations thou shalt give the sign of silence ["The sign of Harpocrates"] and afterward thou shalt perform the adoration that is taught thee by thy Superior. And then do thou compose Thyself to holy meditation.

---

[3] During the evening adoration, one should assume the God-form of Auramoth, and make the sign of "the Goddess Auramoth."

[4] During the midnight adoration, one should assume the God-form of Apophis, and make the sign of "Set fighting."

6) Also it is better if in these adorations thou assume the God-form of Whom thou adorest, as if thou didst unite with Him in the adoration of That which is beyond Him.

7) Thus shalt thou ever be mindful of the Great Work which thou hast undertaken to perform, and thus shalt thou be strengthened to pursue it unto the attainment of the Stone of the Wise, the Summum Bonum, True Wisdom and Perfect Happiness.

THE INVOCATION
OF THE BORNLESS ONE

This is the Preliminary Invocation from *The Goetia*, or *Lesser Key of Solomon*.[1] It is a well-known fact that this was the favorite invocation of Aleister Crowley. This ritual should be performed at least twice monthly by the magician.

In connection with the performance of this particular ritual, one should study "Liber Samekh" which appears as Appendix IV of *Magick in Theory and Practice*.[2] It is highly recommended that the aspiring magician "invoke often," both on the physical and astral planes.

1) The circle should be prepared as in Step 1-A of "A Lunar Invocation." The altar should be prepared in advance, with setup as follows:

• A single white candle should be placed in the east, north, west, and south.

• Each magickal weapon should be on top of the altar in its respective direction.

• The censer in the east, using Abramelin incense.

---

[1]This work was originally published in 1852 as *A Fragment of a Graeco–Egyptian Work upon Magic*, trans. by Charles Wycliffe Goodwin. I suggest this invocation be performed seven days before and seven days after the full moon.
[2]It is there suggested that this ritual be performed once daily for one month, then twice a day for two months, at dawn and dusk, and then three times a day for three months, adding a noontime performance, and lastly, four times a day for four months, adding a midnight performance. If your schedule allows, this system will prove extremely beneficial.

- A vial of Abramelin Oil in the south.

- A bowl of hyssop-treated, natural water in the west.

- A dish of natural salt in the north.

2) The magician should first take the ritual bath in hyssop-treated water, speaking the words of purification at some time while bathing. After bathing, and before entering the circle area, the magician should make the mark of the Rose Cross over the heart in Abramelin Oil, while speaking the words of consecration. Then don the robe, and enter the circle area, moving to the west side of the altar, facing east.

3) Perform the Star Ruby, as outlined in chapter 4.

4) Then light the candles and incense, and move widdershins (counterclockwise) from the west side of the altar to the north side of the altar, face the south and say:

> Thee I invoke, the Bornless one.
> Thee, that didst create the Earth and the Heavens.
> Thee, that didst create the Night and the Day.
> Thee, that didst create the darkness and the Light.
> Thou art ASAR UN-NEFER: Whom no man hath seen at any time.
> Thou art IA-BESZ.
> Thou art IA-APOPHRASZ.
> Thou hast distinguished between the Just and the Unjust.
> Thou didst make the Female and the Male.
> Thou didst produce the Seeds and the Fruit.
> Thou didst form Men to love one another, and to hate one another.
>
> I am ANKH-U-N-KHONSU thy Prophet, unto Whom Thou didst commit Thy Mysteries, the Ceremonies of

KHEM. Thou didst produce the moist and the dry, and that which nourisheth all created Life.

Hear Thou Me, for I am the Angel of PTAH-APO-PHRASZ-RA: this is Thy True Name, handed down to the Prophets of KHEM.[3]

5) (aleph) Then move widdershins (counterclockwise) to the east side of the altar, and pick up the dagger. Hold it on high, face the east and say:

Hear Me:
AR: THIAU: RhEIBET: A-ThELE-BER-SET:
A: BELAThA: ABEU: EBEU: PhI:
ThETA-SOE: IB: THIAU.

Hear me, and make all Spirits subject unto Me; so that every Spirit of the Firmament and of the Ether: upon the Earth and under the Earth, on dry land and in the water; of Whirling Air, and of rushing Fire, and every Spell and Scourge of God may be obedient unto me.

6) Then with the dagger, make the Invoking Pentagram of the Equilibrium of Actives while vibrating EHIEH, and then make the signs of the Portal. Over the top of that pentagram, make the Invoking Pentagram of Air, while vibrating YEHUWAU, and then make the sign of "Shu supporting the sky."

7) (shin) Then replace the dagger to its place on the altar, and move widdershins to the south side of the altar. [make the sign of the Enterer when passing the northeast.] Pick up the wand, hold it on high, face the south and say:

---

[3]All capitalized names should be vibrated. Additionally, when passing the east, one should always make the sign of "the Enterer."

I invoke Thee, the Terrible and Invisible God: Who dwellest in the Void Place of the Spirit:

AR-O-GO-GO-RU-ABRAO: SOTOU:
MUDORIO: PhALARThAO: OOO: AEPE, The Born-
    less One:

Hear me, and make all Spirits subject unto Me; so that every Spirit of the Firmament and of the Ether: upon the Earth and under the Earth, on dry land and in the water; of Whirling Air, and of rushing Fire, and every Spell and Scourge of God may be obedient unto me.

8) Then, with the wand, make the Invoking Pentagram of the Equilibrium of Actives while vibrating EHIEH, and then make the signs of the Portal. Over the top of that pentagram, make the Invoking Pentagram of Fire while vibrating ELOHIM, and then make the sign of "Thoum-aesh-neith."

9) (mem) Then replace the wand to its place on the altar, and move widdershins to the west side of the altar. [Make the sign of the Enterer when passing the east.] Pick up the cup, hold it on high, face the west and say:

Hear Me:
RU-ABRA-IAU: MRIODOM: BABALON-BAL-BIN-
ABAUT: ASAL-ON-AI: APhEN-IAU: I: PhOTETh:
ABRASAX: AEOOU: ISCHURE. Mighty and Bornless
One!

Hear me: and make all Spirits subject unto Me; so that every Spirit of the Firmament and of the Ether: upon the Earth and under the Earth, on dry land and in the water; of Whirling Air, and of rushing Fire, and every Spell and Scourge of God may be obedient unto me.

10) Then, with the cup, make the Invoking Pentagram of the Equilibrium of Passives while vibrating AGLA, and

then make the signs of the Portal. Over the top of that pentagram, make the Invoking Pentagram of Water while vibrating EL, and then make the sign of "Auramoth."

11) (tau) Then replace the cup to its place on the altar, and move widdershins to the north side of the altar. Pick up the disk, hold it on high, face the north and say:

> I invoke Thee:
> MA: BARRAIO: IOEL: KOThA:
> AThOR-E-BAL-O: ABRAUT:

> Hear me: and make all Spirits subject unto Me; so that every Spirit of the Firmament and of the Ether: upon the Earth and under the Earth, on dry land and in the water; of Whirling Air, and of rushing Fire, and every Spell and Scourge of God may be obedient unto me.

12) Then, with the disk, make the Invoking Pentagram of the Equilibrium of Passives while vibrating AGLA, and then make the signs of the Portal. Over the top of that pentagram, make the Invoking Pentagram of Earth while vibrating ADONAI, and then make the sign of "Set fighting."

13) Then replace the disk to its place on the altar.

14) (aleph mem nun) Now, beginning in the north, circumambulate widdershins for six revolutions, making the sign of the Enterer in the east. Stop in the northeast, after the sixth sign, and face the northeast.

15) Then draw the Invoking Pentagram of the Equilibrium of Actives, while vibrating EHIEH.

16) Then make the sign of the "Rose Cross," drawing three circles around the cross.

17) Then perform the signs of L.V.X. [as in chapter 4, figure 5] and say:

> Hear me:
> AUT: ABAUT: BAS-AUMGN: IAK:
> SA-BA-UT: IAO:
>
> This is the Lord of the Gods:
> This is the Lord of the Universe:
> This is He whom the Winds fear.
> This is He, Who having made Voice by His command-
>   ment is Lord of all Things; King, Ruler and Helper.
>
> Hear me, and make all Spirits subject unto Me; so that every Spirit of the Firmament and of the Ether: upon the Earth and under the Earth, on dry land and in the water; of Whirling Air, and of rushing Fire, and every Spell and Scourge of God may be obedient unto me.

18) Then, still facing the northeast, perform the signs of N.O.X. [as in "The Star Ruby" in chapter 4] and then say:

> Hear Me:
>
> IEOU: PUR: IOU: PUR: IAUTh: IAEO: IOOU: ABRASAX: SABRIAM: OO: UU: AD-ON-A-I: EDE: EDU: ANGELOS TON ThEON: ANLALA LAI: GAIA: AEPE: DIATHARNA THORON.
>
> I am He! the Bornless Spirit! having sight in the feet: Strong, and the Immortal Fire! I am He! the Truth! I am He! Who hate that evil should be wrought in the World! I am He, that lighteneth and thundereth. I am He, from whom is the Shower of the Life of Earth: I am He, whose mouth ever flameth: I am He, the Begetter and Manifester unto the Light: I am He, the Grace of the World:

"The Heart Girth with a Serpent" is My Name!

Come Thou forth, and follow Me: and make all Spirits subject unto Me so that every Spirit of the Firmament, and of the Ether: upon the Earth and under the Earth: on dry land, or in the water: of Whirling Air or of rushing Fire: and every Spell and Scourge of God, may be obedient unto me!

19) Then move widdershins to the west, face the east and say:

IAU: SABAU:

Such are the Words!

20) When the time seems right, perform the Star Ruby.

21) Hold your dagger above your head and say, "And now I say unto thee, depart in peace unto thine habitations and abodes—and may the blessings of the highest be upon thee in the name of (vibrate) YEHUWAU, and let there be peace between thee and me; and be thou very ready to come, whensoever thou art invoked and called, either by a word, or by a will or by this mighty conjuration of Magick Art." Then with the butt of the dagger, strike the top of the altar ten times. First 3 times, pause, then 4 times, pause, then 3 times, and say, "I now declare this temple duly closed." Then strike the altar once.

A SHORT TREATISE ON YOGA

Yoga is basically the art of learning "self discipline." Practicing yoga helps teach you exercise control over the body, through the power of the mind.[1] Serious students of Eastern yoga deem it necessary to isolate themselves from the rest of the world, fast frequently, abstain from sexual relations, etc. However, by practicing basic yoga exercises, you may still obtain many positive results, such as increasing the quality and quantity of personal energy, or development of the aura, without depriving yourself of these simple human pleasures.

Many terms of yoga are of Sanskrit descent,[2] and it may be helpful for the student to be aware of these terms. The following are definitions of some basic yoga terms.

1) **Mantra:** a word or combination of words, spoken repeatedly during meditation. It is used to help focus your attention, and to help block out unwanted thoughts. The mantra may or may not have any specific meaning; however it is the sound which should be focused on, not the literal meaning. Some common mantras include AUM, ALLAH, AUM-TAT-SAT-AUM, AUM-MANI-PADME-HUM, AUM- SHIVAYA-VASHI.[3]

---

[1]For the advanced student, it should be noted one last time, that this explanation is directed toward the novice student of western culture.

[2]An ancient Indo-European language.

[3]The meanings of these mantras may be studied in *Book Four*, by Aleister Crowley, who also tells us that the proper way to use a mantra is by first saying it loudly, and as slowly as possible ten times. Then not quite so loudly, and a little faster ten times; and continuing in this manner until there is nothing but a rapid movement of the lips.

Figure 33. Top: The Ibis; Bottom: The Thunderbolt.

2) **Asana:** posture; physical positioning used to help place the body under the control of the mind. Asanas are used in combination with mantras (and also "pranayama," see #6 on this list). Some basic forms of asanas are illustrated in figure 12 (page 55), and figure 33.

• *The God*—sitting in a chair, head up, back straight, knees together, with hands on knees, eyes closed;

• *The Dragon*—kneel, buttocks resting on heels, toes turned back, back and head straight, hands on thighs;

• *The Lotus*—sitting, with heel of each foot at base of the opposite thigh, with sole turned up, palms of hands resting just above knees, thumb and forefinger touching;

• *The Ibis*—stand, hold left ankle with right hand, free forefinger to lips; you should alternately practice right ankle in left hand;

• *The Thunderbolt*—sitting, left heel at anus, right foot poised on its toes, the heel covering genital area, arms stretched out over knees, head and back straight.

3) **Kundalini:** Serpent Fire; awakening of hidden energy in the root chakra, causing surges of auric energy to spontaneously build up, and powerfully ascend along the spine, and through each chakra. This is said to have disastrous results on the undeveloped aura, and consequently, to the unprepared human experiencing kundalini. It would be extremely rare for this to happen spontaneously; although the experienced practitioner will attempt to stimulate kundalini, but only after the proper preparations.

4) **Prana:** means literally "breath."

5) **Yama:** "control."

6) **Pranayama:** obviously "breath control." Some teachers suggest the practice of counting while breathing to insure

long breaths. However, it is just as effective to concentrate on slowing your breathing down. Endeavor to breathe naturally, yet very slowly and regularly. Another method of pranayama is the blocking off of one nostril at a time, by pushing against the side of the nose with one thumb. This is said to lessen the flow of impurities into the body, and may be practiced alternately.

7) **Pratyahara:** the practice of eliminating every thought from the mind. Success depends on the ability to concentrate on total nothingness, and complete emptiness; allowing absolutely no thoughts to enter the mind.

8) **Dharana:** the total concentration on one single point; focusing all of the powers of the mind on one thought, excluding all others. This involves the visualization of a single figure or object to concentrate on, such as a dot or a line.

9) **Dhyana:** successfully mastering dharana results in dyhana. This is the association of the self as the object of concentration, resulting in disassociation with the physical body. One commonly uses the Sun as the object of concentration. The ultimate goal of achieving dhyana is said to be the annihilation of the human ego, freeing the person to pursue "higher" forms of enlightenment.

10) **Samadhi:** perfect union with God. This is supposed to result some time after achieving the annihilation of the ego. One is said to attain perfect peacefulness, to be "one with the universe," the "ultimate feeling." A master of yoga, Yajna Valkya states: "By Pranayama, impurities of the body are thrown out; by Dharana, the impurities of the mind; by Pratyahara, the impurities of attachment; and by Samadhi is taken off everything that hides the lordship of the soul."[4]

---

[4]Aleister Crowley quotes Valkya in *Book Four* (York Beach, ME: Samuel Weiser, 1980) p. 38.

Beginners at yoga should begin by assuming the less difficult postures, such as "The God" asana, and combine that with the practice of pranayama. Teach yourself to breathe very slowly and regularly while in the asana position. In addition, it is advisable to practice the technique of breathing through only one nostril at a time. During one session, close off one side and breathe through the other nostril only, and alternate during the next session.

When you are able to slow down your breathing for a period of fifteen minutes, without moving your body in any way, then attempt to prevent all thoughts from entering your mind, while in the asana. This should not be too difficult if you have successfully mastered the meditation technique outlined in chapter 5. As explained there, while meditating, the body will rebel and send the brain messages, such as to scratch an itch or shift your weight. These must be ignored! Any itch will go away, cramps will subside. Force yourself to stay in that position and ignore the requests of the body.

After achieving success in focusing on absolute emptiness and nothingness, and mastering the different forms of pranayama, begin to use a simple mantra[5] to help focus your attention while meditating. After successfully mastering the simpler asana positions, attempt the more difficult ones. Also use longer mantras after practicing the simpler ones for a period of time. Always seek to expand yourself.

The ability to focus all of your energies on absolute nothingness is known as pratyahara. When you can achieve this state for ten to fifteen minutes without difficulty, then attempt to establish dharana. First use a distant point of light within the emptiness to focus all of your attention on. After several sessions of concentrating on that point, allow it to form a line. After several sessions of concentrating on the line, form a cross to focus on. Continue to expand and grow.

---

[5]Preferably by Crowley's method, as earlier described.

As you can see, yoga exercises are forms of concentrated meditations. Yoga is a step-by-step procedure to teaching yourself to master control over the physical body. This, in turn, strengthens the powers of the mind, and also, strengthens the quality of personal energy. The results of practicing yoga will lead the development of the aura to a fine pitch, in addition to many other positive benefits.

BIBLIOGRAPHY

Achad, Frater. *Anatomy of the Body of God*. Chicago, 1925; New York: Samuel Weiser, 1973.

———. *Q. B. L. or the Bride's Reception*. New York: Samuel Weiser, 1974.

Agrippa, Henri Cornelius. *Occult Philosophy, Bk. IV: Of Geomancy, Magical Elements, the Nature of Spirits, Magic of the Ancients*. Gillette, NJ: Heptangle, 1985; Kila, MT: Kessinger Publishing, 1992.

———. *Three Books of Occult Philosophy or Magic*. Chicago: Hahn & Whitehead, 1898; New York: Samuel Weiser, 1971; Kila, MT: Kessinger Publishing, 1992; St. Paul, MN, Llewellyn, 1993.

Barrett, Francis. *The Magus or Celestial Intelligencer: Being a Complete System of Occult Philosophy*. London: Lackington Allen & Co., 1801; New York: University Books, 1967; New York: Citadel, Carol Publishing Group, 1975.

Butler, W. E. *Magic and the Qabalah*. London: Aquarian Press, 1964: Also published in the combined edition *Apprenticed to Magic and Magic of the Qabalah*. London: Thorson Publishing Group, 1990.

Cavendish, Richard. *The Black Arts*. New York: Putnam, 1967.

Crowley, Aleister. *Book of the Law*. London: First edition privately published by the O. T. O., 1938; York Beach, ME: Samuel Weiser, 1976.

———. *Book Four*. London: Wieland & Co., 1911–1912; York Beach, ME: Samuel Weiser, 1980.

———. *Book of Lies*. London: Wieland & Co., 1913; York Beach, ME: Samuel Weiser, 1981.

———. *The Collected Works of Aleister Crowley*. Boleskine: Society for the Propagation of Religious Truth, 1906; New York: Krishna Press, 1974; Homewood, IL: Yoga Publication Society, 1974.

———. *Goetia: The Lesser Key of Solomon*. Boleskine: Society for the Propagation of Religious Truth, 1904; Chicago: DeLaurence, 1916; New York: Magickal Childe, 1989.

———. *Magick in Theory and Practice by The Master Therion*. Paris: LeCram Press, 1929; New York: Castle Books, n.d.; New York: Krishna Press, 1973; New York: Magickal Childe, 1991.

———. *Magick Without Tears*. St. Paul, MN: Llewellyn, 1973; Phoenix, AZ: New Falcon Publications, 1991.

———. *777 and Other Qabalistic Writings*. York Beach, ME: Samuel Weiser, 1986.

Dee, John. *True and Faithful Relation of Dr. John Dee and Some Spirits*. London: D. Maxwell, 1659; New York: Magickal Childe, 1992.

De Laurence, L. W. *The Great Book of Magical Art, Hindu Magic and Indian Occultism*. Chicago: DeLaurence, 1904.

———. *The Sixth and Seventh Books of Moses*. Trans. by J. Scheible. Carbondale, IL: Egyptian Publishing Co., n.d.

Driscoll, Daniel J., trans. *The Sworn Book of Honourius the Magician*. Gillette, NJ: Heptangle, 1983.

Frazer, James. *The Golden Bough*. London: Macmillan, 1890; New York: St. Martin's Press, 1966.

Godwin, David. *Godwin's Cabalistic Encyclopedia: A Complete Guide to Cabalistic Magick*, 2nd revised and expanded edition. St. Paul, MN: Llewellyn, 1989.

Grant, Kenneth. *The Magical Revival*. London: Frederick Muller, 1972; London: Skoob Books, 1991.

Gray, Eden. *The Tarot Revealed*. New York: Inspiration House, 1960; New York: NAL-Dutton, 1969.

King, Francis. *Modern Ritual Magic: The Rise of Western Occultism*. Garden City Park. NY: Avery Publishing Group, 1989.

———. *Techniques of High Magic: A Guide to Self-Empowerment*. Rochester, VT: Inner Traditions, 1991.

King, Francis, ed. *Astral Projection, Ritual Magic and Alchemy*. New York: Samuel Weiser, 1975; Rochester, VT: Inner Traditions, 1987.

———. *Secret Rituals of the O.T.O.* London: C. W. Daniels Publishing, 1973.

Knight, Gareth. *The Practical Guide to Qabalistic Symbolism*. Cheltenham, England: Helios, 1965; York Beach, ME: Samuel Weiser, 1978.

Levi, Eliphas. *Book of Splendours*. York Beach, ME: Samuel Weiser, 1973.

———. *History of Magic*. Trans. by A. E. Waite. London: Rider, 1913; Los Angeles: Borden Publishing Co., n.d.; York Beach, ME: Samuel Weiser, 1970.

———. *Transcendental Magic: Its Doctrine and Ritual*. Trans. by A. E. Waite. London: Rider, 1896; York Beach, ME: Samuel Weiser, 1968.

Malchus, Marius. *The Secret Grimoire of Turiel*. London: Aquarian Press, 1960.

Mathers, S. L. MacGregor. *The Book of Sacred Magic of Abra-Melin, the Mage*. London: George Redway, 1883; Chicago, DeLaurence, 1932; New York: Dover, 1975.

———. *The Grimoire of Armadel*. York Beach, ME: Samuel Weiser, 1979.

———. *The Kabbalah Unveiled*. London: Routledge & Kegan Paul, 1887; York Beach, ME: Samuel Weiser, 1983.

———. *The Key of Solomon the King*. London: George Redway, 1888; York Beach, ME: Samuel Weiser, 1989.

Porta, John B. *Natural Magic*. London: Thomas Young and Samuel Speed, 1658; New York: Basic Books, 1957.

Regardie, Israel. *Ceremonial Magic: Its Mechanism and Ritual*. London: Aquarian Press, 1980.

———. *The Complete Golden Dawn System of Magic*. Phoenix, AZ: New Falcon, 1991.

———. *The Golden Dawn: An Account of the Teachings, Rites and Ceremonies of the Golden Dawn*. Chicago: Aries Press, 1937; St. Paul, MN: Llewellyn, 1986.

———. *A Garden of Pomegranates: An Outline of the Qabalah*. London: Rider, 1932; St. Paul, MN: Llewellyn, 1970.

———. *The Middle Pillar*. Chicago, Aries Press, 1938; St. Paul, MN: Llewellyn, 1970.

———. *The Tree of Life: A Study in Magic*. London: Rider, 1932; York Beach, ME: Samuel Weiser, 1972.

Sephariel. *The Kabala of Numbers*. Boston: 1914; North Hollywood, CA: Newcastle, 1974; San Bernardino, CA: Borgol Press, 1980.

Shah, Idries. *Secret Lore of Magic*. London: Frederick Muller, 1957; New York: Carol Publishing Group, 1970.

Turner, Robert, trans. *The Arbatel of Magic*. London: 1655; Gillette, NJ: Heptangle, 1979.

Waite, Arthur E. *The Book of Black Magic and Pacts*. London: Redway, 1898; York Beach, ME: Samuel Weiser, 1972.

———. *Book of Ceremonial Magic*. London: Rider, 1911; New York: Carol Publishing Group, 1970.

———. *Holy Kabbalah: A Study of the Secret Tradition of Israel*. London: Williams & Norgate, 1928; New York: Carol Publishing Group, 1976.

———. *The Pictorial Key to the Tarot*. London: Rider, 1910; York Beach, ME: Samuel Weiser, 1973.

Webster's Ninth New Collegiate Dictionary. Springfield, MA: Merriam-Webster, 1989.

Westcott, W. Wynn. *An Introduction to the Study of the Kaballah*. London: J. M. Watkins, 1910; New York: Allied Publications, n.d.

White, Nelson and Anne White, eds. *Lemegeton, Clavicula Salomonis, Or the Complete Lesser Key of Solomon the King*. Fremont, CA: The Technology Group, 1979.

The Talmud: Selections. Translated by H. Polano. London & New York: Frederick Warne, n.d.

The Torah. One source is *The Torah Anthology* by Rabbi Yaakov Culi, translated by Rabbi Aryeh Kaplan. New York & Jerusalem: Maznaim Publishing Co., 1977.

Sepher Yetzirah. Translated by Isidor Kalisch. Gillette, NJ: 1987.

Zohar. Translated by Maurice Simon and Paul Levertoff. Brooklyn, NY: Soncino Press, 1934.

Index

Steve Savedow

ABOUT THE AUTHOR

Steve Savedow was born in Daytona Beach, Florida, on July 19, 1961 at 6:00 P.M. His interest in the occult surfaced early, when he purchased the Crowley Thoth Tarot deck at age 13. At 15 he was initiated into a small wiccan coven, and studied wicca for many years. During his early 20s, he began to study ritual magick and qabala, being strongly influenced by the MacGregor-Mathers translations of *The Kaballah Unveiled*, *The Key of Solomon the King*, *The Book of the Sacred Magic of Abra-melin the Mage*, and the writings of Eliphas Levi and Aleister Crowley.

He has worked as an emergency medical technician, a firefighter, an automotive and marine mechanic, a veterinary assistant, and has also been the drummer for a southern rock band, enjoying a small local club following in his hometown of Daytona Beach. He currently lives with his wife and three daughters near Daytona Beach, and is the owner and operator of Serpents Occult Bookstore in Port Orange, FL. This is his first book.